THE
LOVE OF MARY

THE
LOVE OF MARY

Readings
for
The Month of May

by
D. Roberto
Hermit of Monte Corona

"Let us then serve, praise, honor and love Mary without measure, without bounds, because we shall thus give God an infinite pleasure, and we shall soon become saints, and great saints."

(From page 11)

TAN BOOKS AND PUBLISHERS, INC.
Rockford, Illinois 61105

Approved by the Most Rev. Archbishop of New York, 1856.

First published in 1856 by Edward Dunigan & Brother, Catholic Publishing House, New York, NY.

Reset and published in 1984 by TAN Books and Publishers, Inc. Typography is the property of TAN Books and Publishers, Inc., and may not be reproduced, in whole or in part, without written permission from the publisher.

Library of Congress Catalog Card No.: 83-51545

ISBN: 0-89555-243-4

Printed and bound in the United States of America.

TAN BOOKS AND PUBLISHERS, INC.
P.O. Box 424
Rockford, Illinois 61105

1984

Translator's Preface

Dear Reader: It is with the greatest pleasure that I see this little book about to be circulated through the country. I have long desired to see it translated; and at last, concluded that if I wanted it done, I must do it myself.

The worldly-wise may mock at our devotion to the Mother of God, talk of "Mariolatry," and call us idolaters; but you and I know that what is folly in their eyes, is heavenly wisdom. We are not ashamed to honor her whom God honored, to love her whom our Blessed Redeemer loved, nor to call ourselves children of her who was the Mother of Jesus Christ. If they see this little book, they may throw it aside; yet those whom the world calls ignorant, but God calls wise, will read it, and meditate on the truths it contains. They will find in it consolation and pleasure, and will learn from it to love Mary.

It is addressed to Parthenius, a word of Greek origin, which means one who belongs to the Virgin, and is divided into 31 discourses, or chapters, one of which may be read each day during May, the "Month of Mary."

The good Roberto, who wrote this book, is now in Heaven, and has no need of your prayers; but do not, I pray you, neglect to say at least one "Hail Mary" for the translator.

Publisher's Preface

De Maria numquam satis—"Concerning Mary there is never enough!" This ancient saying of the Church is marvellously brought out in this book, *The Love of Mary.* We can never overestimate the greatness, power, beauty, and sanctity of Mary, the Mother of God.

Where did she get her greatness, her power, her beauty, and her holiness? These are all gifts from God to her; they accompanied her glorious vocation to be the Mother of God and the Mother of the children of God.

Though Mary would be nothing without God, her Creator and Savior (who saved her so completely that He *preserved* her from all stain of sin), through God's almighty power she has been exalted above all the angels and saints. In his book entitled *True Devotion to Mary* St. Louis De Montfort explains with great clarity:

> I avow, with the whole Church, that Mary, being a mere creature that has come from the hands of the Most High, is in comparison with His Infinite Majesty less than an atom; or rather, she is nothing at all, because only He is "He who is." Consequently, that grand Lord, always independent and sufficient to Himself, never had, and has not now, any absolute need of the Holy Virgin for the accomplishment of His will and for the manifestation of

His glory. He has but to will in order to do everything.

Nevertheless, I say that, things being as they are now, that is, God having willed to commence and to complete His greatest works by the Most Holy Virgin ever since He created her, we may well think He will not change His conduct in the eternal ages; for He is God, and He changes not, either in His sentiments or in His conduct.

Thus we can understand the words of the hermit author of this book, D. Roberto, regarding God's dependence upon Mary, His submission and obedience to her, and His veneration of her. God willed to glorify His Name and accomplish His will in the world through Mary. Unlike earthly kings, God in His infinite Majesty is so great that He does not fear to share His greatness with a creature. No matter how many gifts God gives to any creature, He Himself always remains infinitely greater.

Sometimes the idea arises that our worship of God should be "pure" in the sense that we should "go directly to God," without becoming "sidetracked" by any creature. But to go to God through Mary is not to be sidetracked; it is to arrive at our destination *sooner*. If you will, Mary is the detour which brings us to our destination *even sooner* than if we had attempted to go "directly to God" on our own. Pope Paul VI asked:

Could anyone ever think that Marian devotion separates him from the unique and supreme devotion that we give to Christ, and through Christ, in the Holy Spirit, to God our Father? Could he ever say that this devotion

is superfluous, when in fact it is a reflection of
the divine plan for the Mother of Christ? . . .
We are convinced without any doubt that
devotion to Our Lady is essentially joined
with devotion to Christ, that it assures a firm-
ness of conviction to faith in Him and in His
Church which, without devotion to Mary,
would be impoverished and compromised.

God Himself willed to depend upon Mary when He
became man. He shut Himself up in her womb, taking
His nourishment from her body. Our Lord also willed
to perform His first miracle of grace, the sanctification of St. John the Baptist in St. Elizabeth's womb, at
the word of Mary. And He performed His first public
miracle at the request of His Mother—the changing of
water into wine at the Marriage Feast of Cana.
Furthermore, God has willed that all His graces
should pass through Mary's hands. Yet God remains
the Master of creation and grace. To quote St. Louis
De Montfort again:

We must take great pains not to conceive
this dependence as any abasement or imperfection in Jesus Christ. For Mary is infinitely
below her Son, who is God, and therefore she
does not command Him as a mother here
below would command her child, who is
below her. Mary, being altogether trans-
formed into God by grace and by the glory
which transforms all the saints into Him, asks
nothing, wishes nothing, does nothing contrary to the eternal and immutable will of
God. When we read in the writings of Saints
Bernard, Bernardine, Bonaventure and others

that in Heaven and on earth everything, even God Himself, is subject to the Blessed Virgin, they mean that the authority which God has been well pleased to give her is so great that it seems as if she had the same power as God; and that her prayers and petitions are so powerful with God that they always pass for commandments with His Majesty, who never resists the prayer of His dear Mother, because she is always humble and conformed to His will.

God is infinitely merciful. Yet sometimes we find it easier to approach a creature, and a mother. God loves to grant His mercy through His Mother. The Lord complained to Ezechiel that there was no one who opposed His anger: "I sought among them for a man that might set up a hedge, and stand in the gap before Me in favor of the land, that I might not destroy it; and I found none." (*Ezech.* 22:30). If God desires that someone pray and offer love so that He might not be required in justice to strike, who can perform this task better than His own Mother? And "If Moses, by the force of his prayer, stayed the anger of God against the Israelites in a manner so powerful that the Most High and infinitely merciful Lord, being unable to resist him, told him to let Him alone that He might be angry with and punish that rebellious people, what must we not think, with much greater reason, of the prayer of the humble Mary, that worthy Mother of God, which is more powerful with His Majesty than the prayers and intercessions of all the angels and saints both in Heaven and on earth?" (*True Devotion*).

It is the will of God, then, that we should serve,

honor, and love Mary with our whole soul, with our whole strength, and with all tenderness; the more we love her, the more we shall please God. The honor and praise we give to the Virgin Mary pass on to God, her Creator who raised her to such perfection and glory. The worship and honor shown by men to the Mother, through love of the Son, are received by the Son as belonging to Him, since they are offered to the Mother in regard of the Son, and because it is known with what incredible love He loves His Mother.

Mary's great desire is to see us love her Son; therefore, she draws and leads us to God, and does not separate and remove us from Him. She desires all our love that she may give it to her Son. She desires us to be hers, in order that she may make us belong entirely to God.

Our Blessed Lady, being most faithful to her Son, draws and conducts to Him all who approach her, and endeavors to reconcile and unite them more closely with God. Therefore, the more we love Mary, the more we shall love God. There is no shorter, easier, or safer path by which we may attain to the perfect love of God than by a tender and sincere love of Mary. This is the will of God.

Let us then serve, praise, honor and love Mary without measure, without bounds, because we shall thus give God an infinite pleasure, and we shall soon become saints, and *great* saints.

The Publishers
October 19, 1984

Contents

PAGE

TO

The Most Holy Mary
MOTHER OF GOD, AND MOTHER OF FAIR LOVE,

HER MOST HUMBLE AND UNWORTHY SERVANT,
D. ROBERTO,
Camaldolese Hermit of Monte Corona

Most Amiable, Most Sweet, and Most Powerful Queen of Love, how great is my rashness, my presumption! Shall I, a most vile worm of the earth, poor, blind, ignorant, and full of miseries and sins, shall I dare to speak of thee—of thee, most exalted Queen of Angels, Empress of the World, Incomprehensible Light, Most Lucid Sun, Spotless Mirror, Most Pure and Living Temple of the Holy Trinity! Shall I dare to speak and write not only of thee, but also of the love which thou bearest us, and which we should have for thee? I confess, My Lady, that this is the same as "to place my mouth in Heaven," and I should deserve, like the profaners of old, Nadab and Abiu, to be consumed by fire; or to be swallowed by the earth, as the sacrilegious Core, Dathan, and Abiron; or to fall dead, like the irreverent and presumptuous Oza; or, at least, to bear that most just and merited reproof, "Why dost thou declare my justices, and take my covenant in thy mouth?" (*Psalm* 49:16).

It is all true, most true; but then, who can help loving thee? Who can love thee, and yet hold his peace? Who can see himself surrounded and overcome with benefits, and not exclaim, full of holy enthusiasm, "O Love! O Love!"

Most Amiable Virgin, I have received from thy great mercy the light to know, in some measure, thy great merit, thy love for me, and the unheard-of graces with which thou surroundest my whole soul and body; I ought, therefore, to burn, and be consumed by thy love; but alas! I have grown old in the impure flame of earthly affections, and now I know not how to kindle in my heart the flame of thy love. Yet I have thought that by meditating and writing of thee, of thy most excellent prerogatives, of thy great merits, and of thy love, I might succeed in striking some little spark of love for thee from my heart of stone.

May it please God, may it please thee, to grant that the little spark may become a fire that cannot be extinguished, that will consume my heart, and the hearts of all those who may read these pages, the hearts of all men. May the whole world love thee. This is my desire, and to this end is my work directed, small and feeble as it is. Do thou bless my desire, and grant that I may write and speak worthily of thee; and do not permit, that while I open to others the light of truth, I should remain in darkness—that while I point out to others the Fountain of Eternal Life, I should myself perish with thirst.

First Day

"A great thing is love," says Saint Bernard. It is the life of the soul, and a soul without love is as a body without life. "He that loveth not, abideth in death" (1 *John* 3:14), says the holy Evangelist Saint John. Saint Jerome and Saint Bonaventure consider a soul without love an impossible thing. "It is impossible," says the former, "that the soul of man should not love, that it should be without affection" *(Ep. ad Eust.);* and Saint Bonaventure says, "The soul cannot be without love." *(Cap. 2, Solit).* I will even go further and say, it seems that there is nothing in the world, however inanimate it may be, which is not ruled, possessed, and governed by love. Thus the poet attributes love to the stars and the sea. *(Ipsa suas etiam patiuntur sidera flammas; Ipsum etiam credo novit amare mare).*

But how badly, Parthenius, this love is employed, which is the life of the human soul! On how many unworthy objects it is lost! Some love the vile dust of gold; for this they live and breathe; they go without eating, drinking, or sleeping, in order to gain it, and to keep it. They live shut up with it in a perpetual prison, and die with it in their bosom. Others, like foolish butterflies, flutter around the vain splendor of honor, till, after an incessant struggle to obtain it, they are at last consumed by its fatal flame. I speak not of that innumerable multitude of unfortunate beings who, lost in the pursuit of pleasure, waste their wealth, their

1

honor, their life, and their immortal soul, for those objects which, washed and painted on the outside, are but filthy sepulchers within. But there are some yet worse than these; they are those who, becoming foolish and contemptible even in the eyes of the world, bestow their love on objects not only irrational, but even insensible, and sometimes abominable.

Caligula loved a horse to such a degree, that, after keeping him in a gilt stable and feeding him in a golden manger, he made him his colleague in the consulship and pontificate. The Emperor Tiberius passionately loved a serpent; Lucius Crassus a lamprey; Xerxes fell in love with a planetree; Passienus Crispus with a cypress; and an Athenian youth became so distractedly and ardently enamored of a statue of the Goddess of Fortune, that he petitioned the Senate for permission to marry it, promising to endow it with the whole of his immense wealth; and because his strange request was refused, he was so overcome with sorrow that he put an end to his life, and expired at the feet of his statue-love.

Can you imagine greater folly or more beastly frenzy? So far, and even further, does that love, without which it is impossible to live when not well regulated, lead us. In order that we may not also be numbered among fools and madmen, and that it may not be said of us as of them, "They became abominable as the things which they loved" (*Hos.* 9:10), let us regulate our love. To do this we need only make a proper choice of the object to be loved; for, as Saint Augustine assures us, we shall be such as is the object which we love. "If you love the earth, you will be earthly; if you love God, shall I say that you will be a god? I should not dare to say so were it not that God Himself says so in the Holy Scriptures: 'I have said,

you are gods, and all of you sons of the Most High.'"
(Tract. in Ep. ii, Joan).

Now this is precisely my aim, to present you an object worthy of your love; an object on which you may employ all your affections with pleasure and benefit, with honor and glory; to the immense profit and advantage of all your interests, temporal and spiritual; in life as in death; in time and in eternity. It is an object so noble, so great, so rich, so powerful, that you can find none greater under God; so lovely in itself by its beauty and the accumulation of its most excellent perfections; without any mixture of defect or imperfection which might render it less estimable, that even a slight knowledge of it will draw our hearts perforce to love it. It is so full of love for us, so desirous of our love, so interested in all that concerns us, that it seems as though it could not be what it is without us; an object in which you may find all that you can desire. *"In me omnia"*—"In me are all" was the proud motto of the Duke of Brittany, who bore on his shield a wreath of flowers to surpass the pomp of his knights who bore, one a rose, another a lily, a third an anemone, and some one flower and some another. But it belongs more properly to the object which I propose to you; and you may well say, if you have the happiness to love and possess it, "All good things came to me" together with it. *(Wisd.* 7:11).

But perhaps you will say, what object can ever be so precious, so worthy? Can any such be found in the world outside of God? "Far and from the uttermost coasts" is the price of it. *(Prov.* 31:10).

Yes, Parthenius, such an object may be found, and it is so easy to find it that it is sufficient to desire it. "She is easily seen by them that love her, and is found by them that seek her." *(Wisd.* 6:13). From these words you will easily understand of whom I speak: they are said of Wisdom, but the Church applies them to Mary, the Mother of God. This is the object I propose to you to love, which can make you happy, and may worthily occupy your whole heart.

Oh, what an amiable object is this! She it is that steals hearts. "Ravisher of Hearts" is the title given her by Saint Bernard. "She is a sea of sweetness, an ocean of goodness and love, an ever-burning fire consuming all things and changing them into itself." *(S. Dionys. Areopag. ap. Cornel. a Lapid. in 1 Ep. iv. 16)*. With more reason may it be said to her than to Solomon, "Blessed are thy men and blessed are thy servants, who stand before thee always and hear thy wisdom." (3 *Kings* 10:8). She is a sun, says Saint Gregory Nazianzen, which manifests still more its glory and its beauty the more we contemplate it. In fine, she is a treasure in which is found all that can be desired that is good, delightful, glorious, or useful. If you find the Virgin, says Jordan called the Idiot, you will find all that is good. *(In proem. Contempl. B. V.)*.

This, then, is that most amiable object which I present to you, which I counsel you, entreat you, and desire to persuade you to love, if you wish to be happy. But since we cannot love that which we do not know, at least by fame and report, I propose to make you know it, together with all those qualities and perfections which render it amiable, as far as may be compatible with the insufficiency and weakness of my vision, which can ill fix its sight on so luminous a sun without being dazzled by its splendor. And be persuaded that whatever I may say in praise of the Most Holy Virgin, I can never go beyond the truth; for no language, says Saint Basil of Seleucia, can equal the greatness of her dignity. *(Orat. in Assumpt.)*. And Saint

John Damascen asserts that all the tongues in the universe taken together would not be enough to celebrate her praises.

Let us pray this amiable Mother of Wisdom to give me the power to express her praises, and to you the light to understand them, that both you and I may burn with the fire of her love, which shall not be extinguished for all eternity.

Second Day

HOW PLEASING IT IS TO GOD TO HAVE US
LOVE MARY—HOW MUCH HER LOVE
CONTRIBUTES TO OUR SALVATION

At the first step a difficulty and objection may arise: that in consecrating your whole love and affection to the Virgin, who is only a creature after all, you might be defrauding God of that pure and entire love which He requires for Himself alone and undividedly, for which He has given us an express and formal command: "Thou shalt love the Lord thy God with thy whole heart, and with thy whole soul, and with thy whole strength." (*Deut.* 6:5).

The objection is a reasonable one, and you have a right to make it; but be not disturbed, fear not, doubt not. God is indeed jealous of His love, but He is not jealous of the love we bear to Mary; nor can this love be prejudicial to that sanctity and perfection which He desires of us. I may even say, the more we love Mary, the more we shall love God, and the more we shall please Him; and we shall advance in sanctity and perfection in proportion as the love of Mary increases within us. There is no shorter, easier, or more secure way of attaining to the perfect love of God, than that of loving Mary.

The love of God consists, as you well know, in a perfect conformity to His divine will. "If you love me," He says to His apostles, "keep my commandments." (*John* 14:15). Now, the precise will of God is that we

6

serve, honor, and tenderly love Mary. She is, after the sacred humanity of Christ, the most perfect of His works; and what workman is there that is not pleased, that does not desire to have his works admired, praised, and held dear, especially the most excellent of them all—that on which he most prides himself— since the praise and glory of the work redound, and are wholly converted into the praise and glory of the workman? Must it not then be most pleasing to God; must He not desire that we love and esteem that work which He has made to show forth His omnipotence, His infinite wisdom and love, and in which His labor and workmanship are so resplendent and bright, that the saints have termed it "a miracle of the Divine Power?"

God commands us to "obey our prelates, and be subject to them" (*Heb.* 13:17), and to "obey our carnal masters as Christ." (*Ephes.* 6:5). If, then, He wills and commands us to love, honor, obey, and serve our superiors even of this world, what love, obedience, and veneration must He not desire us to show to her who is our Lady and Mistress, the Queen of the World, and who with truth may say: "By me kings reign, and lawgivers decree just things: By me princes rule, and the mighty decree justice?" (*Prov.* 8:15, 16).

She is our Mother, even more really so than our natural mother; Christ gave her to us as such in the person of His beloved John when dying on the cross. As our Mother, she loves us most tenderly; she protects and defends us; provides for us, and helps us in all our necessities, both spiritual and temporal. Imagine, then, what love it must be the will of God that we should render such a Mother—the will of that God who gave us an express command to honor and love our natural parents, even though they love not us:

"Honor thy father and thy mother." (*Exod.* 20:12).

In short, not to enlarge on the innumerable titles which she has to expect of us, if I may so speak, an *infinite* love, she is the Mother, truly the Mother, the Daughter, and Spouse of God Himself—all titles which partake of the infinite, and consequently bear with them and demand an infinite esteem, veneration, and love. It is the will of God that we love and honor His servants as so many gods: "I have said, ye are gods." (*Ps.* 81:6). And can it be His will that we should leave without honor, without service, and without love, His Mother, His Daughter, His Well-beloved Spouse—that Mother, that Daughter, that Spouse to whom He confesses Himself indebted—her from whom He received His humanity—to whom He gave ready obedience, and whom He served in this life—whom He loved, loves, and will love eternally above all His works ("The Lord loveth the gates of Sion, above all the tabernacles of Jacob"—*Ps.* 86:2)—whom He has honored and exalted above all the orders and hierarchies, and who is His only love, His only consolation, His only glory: "One is my dove, my perfect one is but one." (*Cant.* 6:8).

No, do not believe it, but rather be persuaded that it is the will of God that we should serve her, honor her, and love her with our whole soul, with our whole strength, and with all tenderness, and that the more we love her, the more we shall please Him.

But what are the intrinsic reasons why it is so pleasing to God, that we should honor and love His Most Holy Mother? There are two, which I trust will appear to you stronger than all others, and make you resolve to dedicate yourself entirely to the love of Mary.

The first is the honor and glory of God. The primary object of our love and devotion is God, regarded, as theologians say, *terminative,* as our last end; the secondary object is the saints and the blessed, and above all the Most Holy Virgin, who are all regarded *transeunter,* as things belonging to God and directed to God. "The devotion to the saints," says Saint Thomas, "does not terminate with them, but passes to God, inasmuch as it is God whom we venerate in His servants." *(Sum. Theol. II II, q. 82, art. 2, ad 3).*

Now, if this be so (and who does not see that the honor, service, and love we bear to Mary, are the honor and glory, service and love of God Himself?) "all the honor bestowed on the Mother redounds to the Son" *(Hieronym. ad Eustoch.),* and "the praise of the Mother belongs to the Son" *(S. Bern. Homil. 4. super Missus est, c. 1);* "for the honor given to His Mother tends to the praise and glory of the Saviour." *(S. Bonav. in Psalt. B. V. psalm, Si vere utique).* "Let us venerate and love the Most Glorious Virgin Mary," says Father Alexis of Sales, "since the honor and love we bear her, redound wholly to the glory and honor of our Master and Saviour Jesus Christ." And who knows not that all the service done to any saint for the love of God, tends wholly to the glory of God Himself, by whose grace and benefits that saint is what he is?

In honoring, then, the Blessed Virgin as the most excellent and perfect of all creatures, we in reality confess that all those things which render her worthy of our regard and admiration, are derived from His liberality; and we give Him, at the same time, immortal thanks, praising and magnifying Him, who raised a creature, like unto ourselves, to such perfection and glory. We may add that the worship and reverence exhibited by men to the Mother, through love of the Son, are received by the Son as a thing that belongs to Him, since they are offered to the Mother in regard of the Son, and because it is known with what incredible love He loves His Mother.

The second reason is our own profit and advantage, which God wills, desires, and procures for us in all possible manners. The Most Holy Virgin is not one of those creatures that "separate us from God." Oh no! She draws, allures, obliges, and constrains our love, to make thereof a most pleasing gift to God: she wishes us hers, that she may make us belong entirely to God; she wishes us to love her, that she may make us enamored of her Son; and therefore she draws and leads us to God, and does not separate and remove us from Him. As says the pious author of a work on the love and worship of the Mother of God, "The devotion and love of the Son increases with that which men bear the Mother, because the Mother, being most faithful to the Son, draws and conducts to Him all who approach her, and endeavors to reconcile and unite them more closely with God." *(In arte pie amandi et colendi Deipar. cap. 7).* And by this you may see how great the advantage is to ourselves, and therefore I say that the more we love Mary, the more we shall love God, and that there is no shorter, easier, or safer path by which we may attain to the perfect love of God, than a tender and sincere love of Mary.

Pelbartus asks if those persons sin, who seem to venerate the Most Holy Virgin more fervently and devoutly than Christ. *(Pelb. apud Wickmann, Sabbat. Marian, c. 13).* To this question, Wickmann replies that certainly, and without any rashness, we may believe that the Holy Ghost wishes to inflame many

with a special devotion to the Most Holy Mother of
God, that by her merits they may obtain everlasting
salvation, and lead others, by their example, to a like
affection of piety and devotion. *(Ibid).*

If, then, you wish to love God, and to love Him ardently and constantly, love Mary, and love her with
strength and perseverance. If you wish to be holy,
and if you wish to become so quickly and easily, love
Mary, and love her tenderly and fervently. Of the
love we should bear her, I shall speak more in the
last chapter. Pay no attention to those who, guided,
as we may piously believe, by a good zeal towards
God, but certainly with little piety and devotion
towards the Blessed Virgin, either destroy, or in
some manner diminish her most beautiful praises, or
wish to reform or else entirely abolish certain
religious practices in her honor, which the piety of
the faithful, or the most ancient custom of the
Church has introduced, and hitherto continued. But
consider that there is no rule nor measure in the
honor and love of the Virgin, because she surpasses,
transcends all praise, all honor, according to the
words of Saint John Damascen; and therefore Saint
Ambrose, and Andrew of Crete assert that only God
can sufficiently and worthily praise the Most Holy
Virgin. *(St. Ambrose, lib. i. de Virg., Andreas Cret.).*

Let us then serve, praise, honor, and love Mary
without measure, without bounds, because we shall
thus give God an infinite pleasure, and we shall soon
become saints, and great saints.

O Mother of Beautiful Love! Most perfect work of
God! Our Most Loving Mother! Most Beloved
Mother, Daughter and Spouse of God; when, oh,
when shall we be inflamed with thy love? When
shall our hearts be consumed by its fire? Separate a

single ray from that divine fire that burns in thy breast, and cast it powerfully into our hearts, that they may also burn and be entirely consumed—a holocaust of that love which they owe to thee, which they owe to God, and that they may be thus purified from those stains which the impure flames, with which they have hitherto been surrounded, have left upon them. Do this through thy mercy, and do it soon.

Third Day

HOW EASY IT IS TO LOVE MARY, AND HOW
MUCH SHE IS PLEASED WITH, AND DESIRES
OUR LOVE

The promised land, said the explorers sent thither
by Moses, is a most fertile and delightful country,
flowing with milk and honey; but to reach it and
possess it is not possible for us, because it is defended
by giants and impregnable fortresses. "We came into
the land to which thou sentest us, which in very deed
floweth with milk and honey, as may be known by
these fruits. But it hath very strong inhabitants, and
the cities are great and walled. We saw there the race
of Anak." (*Numb.* 13:28, 29). It seems to me,
Parthenius, that I hear you discourse in the same manner: Mary is the Land of Promise; a Land Most
Delightful and Most Fruitful of all good; a Land that
overflows with much more than that milk and honey.
This is most true: no one can doubt it. "She is the Land
of Promise" (*S. Bern. Serm. 3, super Salve Regina),*
"flowing with milk and honey." *(S. August. Serm. 100,
de Temp).* But can anyone reach her, or obtain her
love? The wings of the purest dove or the loftiest
eagle could not suffice. Can I fly so high? Can I, a vile
worm, full of misery and sin, aspire to love, and be
loved by the Queen of Angels, by the Mistress of the
Universe, by purity, by sanctity itself? Oh! I dare not
even think of it. But be not disheartened, Parthenius;
what will you say if I show you that it is a very easy

13

thing to love and to be loved by the Most Holy Virgin; that she even ardently desires, seeks, wishes to love you and to be loved by you? I am most sure, that if I make it so easy to you, you will no longer have any excuse for not loving her. Listen to me, and then tell me if you remain unconvinced.

Nothing is easier to man than love, because the heart has neither enjoyment nor life without it; this we have already seen and proved, and everyone is a witness of this to himself. Moreover, it is the same thing to see, to contemplate a good and amiable object, and to love it, because we feel ourselves carried away, and borne almost towards it. Now, if Mary be that object so amiable, that a more amiable may not be found among creatures, what obstacle or impediment shall delay, hold back, and detain our heart from running and flying to her? Even a little knowledge of her, such as may be obtained by reading, by hearing, and by meditating on her incomparable perfections, her benefits and her love, suffices to set us on fire, and make us melt towards her.

Even when she was in this world, in a most advanced age, the people crowded to see her. "Great is the concourse of people desiring to see and hear the Queen of Heaven" *(S. Ign. apud Joann, Viguer, 75, 4)*, wrote the blessed martyr Ignatius to the Evangelist Saint John; and Saint Denis the Areopagite considered himself most happy to be presented to her by the same holy Evangelist. What attractions, then, must she now possess from that glory, from which the great endowments of her most beautiful body, and of her most innocent soul, have received the last consummation of perfection? Let those fortunate souls instruct you, whose hearts, after contemplating for a short time this Most Luminous Sun, were so inflamed and consumed by its celestial fire, that to give vent to their seraphic ardor, one calls her "Captivator of Hearts," as Saint Bernard; another, like Saint Bonaventure, "My Heart, My Soul," and Saint Ephraim of Syria, "The Strong and Sweet Hope of My Soul." Saint Anselm, beside himself with love, exclaims: "O Most Beautiful and Lovely Mary, where dost thou hide thyself from the eyes of my heart? Wait for a poor, weak soul which follows after thee, and hide not thyself from a heart which seeks thee, and sees thee but little."

You cannot believe that she is deaf to these voices, or that, with haughty greatness, she sees not, or heeds not the prayers and tears of those who love her and seek her. She knows all, she sees all, even the least motions of our soul; and oh! How pleasing and acceptable they are to her! She knows well how to return our love with equal love—with equal love? Ay, with a love inestimably greater; with a love which cannot be surpassed, cannot be equalled. "I know, My Lady," said Saint Peter Damian to her, "I know that thou art most kind, and that thou lovest us with an invincible love." *(Serm. de Nativ. B.V.).* In a transport of love, the blessed Alphonsus Rodriguez, of the Society of Jesus, thus addressed her: "O My Most Amiable Lady, I love thee more than I love myself; but alas! Thou dost not love me as I love thee." "Not so, my Alphonsus," she answered; "I love thee more than thou canst love me; and know," she continued, "that thy love is as far from mine, as is earth from Heaven." "Oh, sweet contest of love!" adds the author who relates it, "in which to be conquered or to conquer, is equally desirable and glorious; but in which she must conquer, who is the most powerful in loving, whose love is not only more tender, but also stronger and more effectual."

(Burghes, in Societ. Mar.).

But this Most Loving Queen not only is pleased with and returns our love, but she ardently desires and solicits it, most sweetly inviting and powerfully drawing us to her love. To her are well applied those words of Wisdom: "She is easily seen by them that love her, and is found by them that seek her. She preventeth them that covet her, so that she first showeth herself unto them. He that awaketh early to seek her, shall not labor, for he shall find her sitting at his door. . . . For she goeth about seeking such as are worthy of her; and she showeth herself to them cheerfully in the ways, and meeteth them with all providence." (*Wisdom* 6:13, 17). "I am the mother of fair love, and of fear, and of knowledge, and of holy hope." (*Ecclus.* 24:24). "Put me as a seal upon thy heart, as a seal upon thy arm." (*Cant.* 8:6). "Give me thy heart," she says to you, "give me thy heart, and I will give thee mine." You will not lose by the exchange; but oh! How much you will gain!

But she complains, that she calls on those that are deaf, that her love is not returned, that it is contemned, that she is rejected for the most unworthy objects. "Be astonished, O ye heavens, at this!" she cries out with Jeremiah; "they have forsaken me, the fountain of living water, and have digged to themselves cisterns, broken cisterns, that can hold no water." (*Jerem.* 2:12, 13).

But yet, you will say, it is those chosen souls, immaculate and holy, those chaste and innocent doves, and high-soaring eagles, that have wings to fly; but can I, a wretch, full of misery and sin, can I hope that this Sublime Queen will deign, I will not say, to love me, but even to cast an eye upon me? Yes, Parthenius, she goes about seeking for lovers; and the further we are from her, the more she approaches us in seeking us; the more wretched we are, the more she pities us, and our very miseries force that loving heart to relieve us, and to love us still more tenderly. She would not be the Queen of Mercy, if in her kingdom there were no objects of mercy; and to such, more than to any others, she says: "Come to me, all ye that are burdened, and I will refresh you." "Come to her," says Saint Bonaventure, "ye that labor and are burdened, and she will refresh your souls. 'Come over to me, all ye that desire me, and be filled with my fruits.'" (*Ecclus.* 24:26). "Approach unto me, all you who desire my love, and I will not reject you, I will not despise you, but will heap upon you those goods with which I abound through my greatness and my noble generation, which made me to be the Mother, Daughter, and Spouse of God. And happy is the soul that yields himself to such sweet invitations, and, from an ungrateful enemy, becomes a faithful friend; from a stranger, becomes a servant; and from an unfaithful one, becomes a most dear and faithful spouse." *(S. Laurent. Justin, de cast, con. verb. et anim. c. xxi).*

"However great may be a man's sins," said this Most Amiable Lady to Saint Bridget, "if he return to me with his whole heart, and with true amendment, I am immediately ready to receive him; neither do I consider how much he has sinned, but with what intention and will he returns. I am called by all the Mother of Mercy, and truly the mercy of my Son hath made me merciful; and he is miserable, who will not, when he can, approach mercy." *(Sta. Brigit. in Revelat. lib. 2. c. 23).*

What say you now, Parthenius? Are you yet convinced that it is very easy to love Mary, that your love

pleases her above all things, that she desires, ardently
desires it, and goes diligently in search of it? Are you
persuaded that she keenly feels, that it pains her not
to be loved, and that she regards not, cares not for the
past vileness, misery, faithlessness, and ingratitude of
him who sincerely wishes and resolves to love her?
Yes, certainly you are convinced; you are persuaded
of this. Take courage, then, and strong resolution. Let
us love her who so greatly loves us, so greatly desires
our love, our good. Oh! Ungrateful and foolish that we
are; we have perhaps been lost in the pursuit of one
who fled from us, who despised us, and sometimes
even hated us; and shall we not yield ourselves to the
love of her who has so long sought for, and so highly
prizes our poor heart?

"O Great Virgin, singularly chosen by God, and elevated above all in Heaven, how admirable and how
lovely are thy eyes, and their most pleasing rays! Turn
them upon us. Attract and draw us to thee, and obtain
for us amendment of life, increase of grace, and the
possession of eternal glory." (*S. Bonavent*).

Fourth Day

HOW SWEET THE LOVE OF MARY IS

Love is so sweet a pleasure that it moves and almost forces all hearts, even the hardest and the most austere. "We are all moved by pleasure," said the Latin orator *(Cic. i. de Leg.)*; and Cato says, pleasure is the bait of the wicked, by which men are caught as fishes with a hook. Cicero calls pleasure a most sweet tyrant *(Cic. de Offic. ii),* and Aristotle hesitated not to declare that pleasure is by nature something divine implanted in mortals. *(Lib. 6 Ethic. c. xiii).* You cannot have believed, or even imagined, that the love of Mary is without pleasure, and therefore insipid to the corrupt palate of man. No, you will find no greater pleasure on earth than in the love of Mary, always excepting the love of God. The love of Mary, it is true, rejects, hates, and abhors such pleasure as is contrary to the law, to honesty of morals, and to her most holy purity and innocence. But, oh, with how many innocent joys and delights does she fill the soul, and sometimes even the body of those who love her!

You well know, Parthenius, and perhaps have unfortunately experienced, how uneasy, bitter, and unhappy is the carnal love of creatures; to how many labors, fatigues, inconveniences, sufferings, and ignominies it condemns one. A man begins by loving an object which he believes in every way amiable, but by little and little he discovers very considerable defects and imperfections, either natural or moral, which render it distasteful, miserable in its nature, most vile in its condition, incapable and wholly insufficient to console him in his labors, to help him in his fatigues, to comfort him in his troubles, to liberate him from dangers, to counsel him in his doubts, and to alleviate his miseries. He then finds it to be an insatiable leech which sucks up and devours all he has, or a proud Aman demanding his adoration, and at the same time scorning and despising him; a fraudulent and deceitful syren, who entices him by flatteries, and kills him by infidelity, faithlessness, and treachery; a merciless Pharaoh, who condemns him to insupportable fatigues, sufferings, and labors.

Suspicions, jealousies, anxiety, infamy, persecution, hatred, most fierce enmity, are the portion of the soul that is possessed by worldly love. And even when everything goes on prosperously (which, however, is impossible), still the fear of losing the object beloved, the thought of having to separate from it one day, is ever a sharp thorn, a cruel knife to the heart of the lover. And yet, who would believe it? Such a lover rejoices, exults, and esteems himself most happy in his misfortune, if he finds, or believes and flatters himself he shall find, a return of his love.

Think now what pleasure, what joy, and what content the heart feels that truly loves Mary. He considers and knows that he loves and is loved by a Lady so sublime, so lofty, so great, so noble, that he sees the knees and the proud necks of all the greatest potentates of the world bend to her as the Empress of the Universe. And oh, blessed that I am, he cries, this is she whom I love, and by whom I am loved! He finds her full and overflowing with the wisdom of the Son, with which she sees, knows, and penetrates all things; she holds in her hand the omnipotence of the Father, and all the treasures of the Divinity, inflamed and wholly penetrated with the immense and inextinguishable fire of divine love.

Oh, what can I ever want? What can I fear, he adds. My Queen, who loves me with an invincible love, knows and sees all my necessities, my troubles, my miseries, and my most minute wants. All is possible to her, all is known to her. She does everything to counsel and comfort me, to help and assist me. And oh, happy man that I am! Except for the human nature of her Son, there is neither in the world, nor out of it, neither on earth nor in Heaven, created beauty more perfect, more lasting. She knows my love, sees my thoughts and my heart; she hears my sighs, listens to my supplications, accepts and is pleased with my affections; she gratefully returns my love, and she loves me much more than I can love her; she excuses my failings, compassionates my weakness, and is not wearied and annoyed even by imperfections, but she continues most constantly to love me, to defend me, and to help me, although ungrateful, although faithless. She knows who are my enemies, both visible and invisible; she sees their plots, their snares, their violence, and she fights for me, helps me, defends me, and gives me a complete victory over them.

If I am afflicted, troubled, and laboring, she guides, consoles, comforts, and rejoices me. If I am oppressed by poverty, I confidently await the necessary supplies from my Heavenly Treasurer. If I lie languishing with sickness or grief, I turn to her and she extends to me the proper remedy. If calumnies or my past irregularities seem to blacken my name and stain my good reputation, she pitying hastens to my relief, and frees me from all infamy. I see myself loaded with miseries, defects, and sins, and therefore an object of hatred to the Divine Justice; but she is My All-Power-ful Advocate, who defends my cause at the Divine Tribunal; she appeases my Judge, who is still her Son; she restores me to His grace, and makes Him pardon me every excess, forgive me every punishment. Perhaps I shall lose confidence in my last agony, doubtful of my salvation, and assailed by my fiercest enemies? No, I shall not fear, for she will be with me; she will be my comfort, my sure defence. And after death do not those atrocious torments, which must at least purge me from my faults, terrify me? No, they give me no apprehension; for either they will be mitigated and shortened by My Dear Protectress, or I shall be entirely delivered from them. And then, blessed and happy that I shall be! I shall enjoy the good fortune to be united to My Lady without fear of losing her, and with her my everlasting beatitude.

And must not a soul which understands all this, a heart moved by such and so great affection, swim in an ocean of joy and content? If you will not believe me, ask those happy souls who have felt it and who now feel it. Hear Saint Bernard, who exclaims, "O Great, O Merciful, O Most Amiable Mary, thou canst not be named without enkindling love; the thought of thee consoles the affections of those who love thee: Thou never returnest to our memory without that sweetness that is natural to thee." *(S. Bernardus apud Liguori. Glor. Mar.).* Listen to Saint Anthony of Padua, who says, "She is joy to the heart, honey to the mouth, and sweet melody to the ear." *(Anton. Pav. apud Bonav. Spec. c. viii).* Blessed Henry Suso cries out, "O Mary, what must thou thyself be, since thy name alone is so sweet!"

But, above all, give ear to Saint Bonaventure, whose enamored heart, at every moment transported with love, breaks forth in a thousand ways: "How great is the multitude of thy sweetness, O Lady, which thou hast prepared for them that love thee and hope in thee!" *(S. Bonav. Stim. Amor. p. 3. c. xvi)*. "How amiable are thy words to them that love thee, how sweet are the drops of thy graces!" *(Idem in Psal. Domine in virtute)*. "Thy spirit is sweeter than honey, and thy inheritance is sweeter than honey and the honeycomb." *(St. Bona. in Ps. Verba mea)*. "Her memory is sweeter than honey and the honeycomb, and her love is sweeter than all spices." *(Id. in Ps Notus in Judaea)*. "She has taken from my heart all sadness and grief, and has inundated it with her sweetness." *(Id. in Ps. Voce mea)*. "O My Sweet Lady, the mere thought of whom sweetens every affection, whose beauty rejoices the eye of my mind! O Lady, who ravishest hearts by thy sweetness, hast thou not stolen my heart? Where, I pray thee, hast thou placed it? Tell me, that I may be able to find it. Hast thou placed it in thy bosom? Perhaps thou hast placed it there that thou mightest warm and inflame it. O Ravisher of Hearts, when wilt thou restore me my heart? Wherefore dost thou steal the hearts of the simple? Why dost thou do violence to thy friends?" *(Id. in Stim. Amor. p. 5. c. xix)*.

Oh, he indeed had felt how sweet is the love of Mary; but you shall also experience this, and so shall I, if we but make a trial, however slight it may be.

God, the provident Author of Nature, most attentive to whatever conduces to our good, has given all things a special natural inclination to all that is necessary and proper for them, and therefore has placed a singular pleasure and delight in the actions necessary for the sustenance of the individual, or the conservation of the species. In the same manner has He acted in the order of grace, which is much more necessary for us. He knows what great good and advantage the love of Mary, His Most Holy Mother, is to us, and has therefore instilled into us, even from our most tender years, a particular confidence, tenderness, and inclination towards her, and has infused into her devotion, service, and love, I know not what sweetness and delight, which ravishes us towards her, and which goes on, ever increasing more and more, as our confidence and love towards her increase. I shall bring no other proof of this than yourself and your own experience, and I am sure that, if you do not wish falsely to deceive yourself, you will frankly confess that you have felt in yourself, even from the cradle, if I may say so, a special tenderness towards this Amiable Lady, and so great sweetness of affection and piety in her service, that it dilates your heart, and fills you with consolation, much more than all the delights and pleasures you have ever felt on this earth.

Nor is this special providence of grace without a reason, since, as I have before said, the service and love of Mary are of much more importance to the life of the soul, than any external action to the preservation of the life of the body; and therefore God has willed that the interior delight of her devotion should be much greater than any pleasure of the senses. Or, rather, Mary, according to Richard of Saint Victor, makes her servants feel all sweetness and delight, even sensibly. "In Mary," he says, "each sense finds its own pleasure, its own delight." It is her thought and her care to render happy and contented those who love her, and to compensate them a hundred and a thousandfold for the pleasures of which they deprive themselves for love of her. The experience of many may serve as a proof of this.

The blessed Peter, Abbot of Citeaux, and disciple of Saint Bernard, desired the pleasure of contemplating, with his corporal eyes, that Incomprehensible Beauty which constitutes a paradise of itself, and this Kind Princess did not refuse to comfort him and grant him the happiness of seeing her even in this life. Marsillus, Bishop of Tuscia, while reciting the *Ave Maria* in the church of Saint Severinus at Cologne, tasted in his mouth a sweetness beyond anything of this world. *(Nieremberg, Aff. Mar. c. xxi).* A Cistercian monk, called Thomas, also desired to see her. Perhaps you think she refused him this consolation. She did not wait long, and if she waited at all, it was only to make him doubly blessed. She sent Saint Catharine and Saint Agnes to announce to him the most fortunate visit he was about to receive from the Queen of Angels, and to dispose him for it by their presence; shortly afterwards she descended from the open heavens, surrounded by light and by the celestial hosts, so full of majesty, grace, and beauty, that the mind of man could conceive nothing more worthy and more noble. After comforting him with words of sweetest consolation, accompanied by the hosts of angels, she left him so overjoyed with her kindness that, unable to restrain the torrent of his raptures, he fainted away, and was found a few hours afterwards almost lifeless.

What will you say, Parthenius, to this? Does Mary know how to repay those who love her; to make her faithful servants abound with pleasure? Would you not renounce all the pleasures of this world for a single one of these consolations?

But you will say these graces are most extraordinary, and reserved only for the most holy and perfect souls. I should never presume to think of obtaining such favors, and it would be utter rashness in me even to expect them. You are right, Parthenius; but do you believe that these fortunate souls became all at once so familiar and dear to this Great Princess? Not so; but by serving and honoring her, gradually through her assistance they became saints, and then merited such special graces. Serve, honor and love Mary incessantly, and I assure you that if you come to possess her grace and her love—as I have shown you to be very easy—she, that is not scant of her graces nor parsimonious of her favors, will give you to enjoy similar delights, and perhaps even greater, if your love be greater. And if you do not feel these sensible pleasures, you certainly shall not want the consolation and spiritual joy which incredibly surpasses all sensible and worldly delights. Make the experiment, and you are sure to be satisfied with the result.

Fifth Day

One of the most certain effects of sensual love is that it entirely destroys, or at least greatly diminishes, honor and reputation. As soon as one is possessed by this spirit he commences to lose all sense; wise and rational before, he now falls into such baseness and excesses, that he can no longer be considered any better than a crazy fanatic; and because he generally tramples underfoot all law, human and divine, his soul, and God, to obtain his ends and carry out his perverse designs, he is commonly esteemed not only foolish, but even impious and beyond hope. Remember David, remember Samson, think of Solomon and Ammon, and not to go so far back, you may have heard of Raymond Lullus, called "the enlightened Doctor." He was so fascinated by a lady before his conversion, although his love was not returned, that one day, following after her, he happened to enter the church where she was, on horseback, to the surprise and scandal of all the people, who detested and cursed him as foolish, mad, and impious. *(Leg. Franc. vita).* These are the sweet fruits and wonderful effects of foolish love.

But such are not the effects of the love of Mary. She is that Wisdom that dwells in counsel and is present in learned thoughts (*Prov.* 8:12); and since she makes her lovers resemble her, he that loves her regulates his thoughts, his affections, his words, his motions, and all his actions by the rule of that Most Prudent, Most Wise, and Most Holy Model which, daily rendering him wiser and holier, makes him also more worthy to be admired and commended, and consequently honored and glorious before the world and before Heaven. "Take hold on her," says the Holy Ghost in the book of Proverbs, "and she shall exalt thee: thou shalt be glorified by her." (*Prov.* 4:8).

Endeavor to procure so rich a gem, and it will raise you to immortal honors; wherefore it was well said by Saint Peter Damian, "It is the greatest glory to live under the shield of thy protection"; and Saint Bonaventure invites us to go in search of her even from our youth, assuring us that she will make us glorious in the sight of all the people. (*S. Bonavent. Psalm In Domino confide*). All the saints of Heaven are authentic witnesses of this, of whom you will not find even one that was not most devout to the Queen of the World. Behold them now glorified in Heaven, and honored upon our altars here on earth.

But she does not wait till after their death to render them glorious, she wishes them to be honored even in this life. Thus the most noble and generous Saint Alexis, for love of Mary, left his bride the very night before his marriage. He lived in Edessa unknown to the world, intent only on venerating and loving Mary, his Dear Lady, in an image of her that was honored in that city; not bearing to see him so humbled and unknown to the whole world, Mary one day made known who he was, relating his merits and praises; so that, being greatly honored by the world, his humility made him fly from that city to live and die an abject and unknown menial in his father's house.

And this is not all. Mary is so desirous of honoring

them that love her, that she takes upon herself their honor, even as regards worldly appearances.

Gualtier de Criqui Birbach, a most devout servant of Mary, was one day to appear in a tournament, to which he had been invited as being the most valiant knight of the country. While on his way, he stopped at a church to hear Mass, and thus the hour of the tournament passed without his arriving in time. As soon as he perceived how late it was, he arose and hurried to the field, reflecting on not having kept his promise and the loss of his reputation to follow. How great was his surprise to meet crowds of people proclaiming the praises of Gualtier, the victor in that day's tournament; and he was soon after joined by his friends, congratulating him and praising his skill and his valor. He was then certain that his Most Loving Lady had not suffered the destruction of his honor, but had sent one of her heavenly champions to fight and conquer for him. Could anyone have a more tender care and desire for our reputation and honor?

I should never finish, and should perhaps weary you, Parthenius, if I should relate to you the innumerable examples of the care that Mary takes of the honor of her servants and her lovers; but there is one which I cannot omit, and from it you may infer the excess of her attention not only to preserve his honor and reputation, but even to glorify and honor him after he had lost it with his life on an infamous gibbet, deservedly due to a thousand crimes committed by him in life; and this in recompense of only a very slight service rendered her.

A famous robber had settled upon the Alps of Trent. His name was become formidable by robberies and murders. He had the good fortune to meet a religious priest, who out of gratitude to him for sparing his life, instructed him and counselled him to practice devotion to Mary, to fast in her honor on Saturday, and on that day to abstain from all robberies and outrages upon travellers; assuring him that if he did so, he would be converted and saved. The robber, who had before despaired of his salvation, accepted this good advice, and faithfully followed it, binding himself by a vow to do so. Accordingly, when a large band of soldiers, sent by the magistrates of Trent, who would no longer permit his robberies and murders to pass unpunished, discovered his retreat and surrounded his men, he suffered himself to be taken and bound without any resistance, because it was Saturday, and he would not violate his oath. He was conducted to Trent and brought before the judge, who, taking pity on his gray hairs and declining age, wished to commute the punishment of death into some other.

But the robber, whose heart was moved by divine grace through the intercession of Mary, protested that he wished rather to be punished by men with temporal death in this world, than to be condemned by God to eternal death in the next. Being, in consequence, condemned and led to the block to be beheaded, he made a public confession of his crimes with such sorrow and contrition, that all who stood around wept out of sympathy with him. The sentence was then executed, and he was beheaded and buried dishonorably in the common grave of criminals. But the Loving Lady, for whose sake the good robber had sometimes abstained from evil, would not suffer the memory of her servant to remain even one day dishonored. That very night, while the wicked were perhaps insulting his name with a thousand reproaches, and the good, for the most part, remembered him with expressions of charitable pity, a great light was seen over the place where he was buried, and the sentinels who kept watch on the walls of Trent were commanded, with a loud voice, to go to the bishop and tell him to give honorable burial to this servant of Mary, in a certain church dedicated to her in that city.

This wonderful event became public in the morning, and the bishop, being informed of what had occurred, went in procession, accompanied by all the clergy and crowds of people, to disinter the corpse, which showed no signs of the sentence which had been executed, all those marks of his disgrace having disappeared. Carried almost in triumph to the church, the obsequies were most solemnly celebrated, and the people honored and venerated him as a saint, admiring and praising the great goodness of Mary, who can so greatly honor and exalt infamous robbers and assassins after a wicked life and shameful death.

O Glory of Jerusalem! O Joy of Israel! O Honor of Our People! How honored are thy friends! Oh, what care thou takest of their reputation in the eyes of the world, even after death, and when they have lost it by their infamous disorders and crimes! Since thou takest our honor in this world so to heart, may our glory be yet dearer to thee in the world to come, that we may there give glory to God and to thee for all ages.

Sixth Day

THE DIGNITY AND GREATNESS OF THE
BLESSED VIRGIN

Having seen the great happiness, glory, and utility of the love of Mary, which will also still further appear from the chapters which follow, we shall now, Parthenius, consider the amiable qualities of Mary, in order that we may become acquainted with this most worthy object of our love, that we may consecrate to her our whole heart and all our affection. The first of these qualities is her great nobility and dignity.

Nobility, Parthenius, is so brilliant a light that it almost dazzles the sight, and makes the spectator bow in submission and reverence. But if it is united with dignity, majesty, and the greatness of high rank, it prostrates its adorers as with a thunderbolt to the earth, and exacts their most profound esteem, love, and worship; they often sacrifice to it not only their substance, but even their health and life. A few instances from history will prove my assertion.

In Arabia Felix, if the king was maimed, all his household were deprived of the same member, "considering it," as says Diodorus Siculus, "an unworthy thing that the king should be lame and the servants should not limp." *(Diod. Sic., lib. 3. c. 10)*. In Ethiopia, on the death of their princes, their servants and wives were glad to be buried with them. *(Athenag., lib. 6, c. 6)*. When Xerxes was in danger of perishing from a sudden storm, the pilot commanded the ship to be lightened; immediately the gentlemen of his suite, anxious to preserve the life of their prince, making him a profound inclination, jumped into the sea. Solimaun once stood on a balcony looking out upon the garden, reading a letter, when it dropped from his hand; a slave, who observed it, to his own imminent risk jumped from a very high window, regained the letter, and presented it to his master. *(Histor. Ottom.).* More celebrated is the deed of the famous Zopirus, the favorite of Darius Hystaspes of Persia, who, seeing the obstinate resistance made by the city of Babylon besieged by his king, cut off his own nose and ears, and all wounded and covered with blood, presented himself before the city, pretending that he had been thus maltreated by Darius; and being well received, and even made general, he opened to Darius, his king, the gates of the city, which could not have been taken without such an artifice.

See how far the esteem, respect, and love, which is given to nobility, dignity, and greatness, may go. But, Parthenius, what nobility, what dignity, what majesty, what greatness can be compared with that of the Mother of God? Let us cast a glance upon it, since it has not yet been granted, and will not be for all eternity granted, even to the minds of the highest angels, fully to understand it; and if we are not dazzled and prostrated by so great a light, it must be said that we are either blind or senseless.

I know not if there ever was, or ever can be found on the earth, greater nobility than that of Mary, even considered only in respect to her human lineage and descent. The Gospel assures us she is "of the house and family of David"; and she was descended from the first great patriarchs—Abraham, Isaac, Jacob, and Juda. David, the great king of Israel, with all his posterity, which was propagated through full 14 monarchs, united the sacerdotal with the royal blood. Let human pride boast, if it can, a brighter or more ancient nobility than this, which is the least of the sublime praises of Mary; "but let every creature be silent and tremble, and hardly dare look upon the immensity of so great dignity." *(Petr. Damian, Serm. i. de Nativ. Virg.).*

Yes, let us cast down our eyes, Parthenius, if we do not wish to be blinded by the splendor of the divine nobility and immense dignity of our Great Princess. She is the Daughter, and Spouse, and Mother, and True Mother of the great God of the universe. She is the Daughter, yes, the True Daughter of God, eternally regarded by God with immense affection and love, and with paternal fondness, above all the creatures ordained to serve her, to honor her, and to love her for all eternity to come; born in time of God, the True Daughter of Grace and of Love, and therefore preserved from all stain of sin that could render her the child of wrath and malediction, like all the other children of Adam; Daughter preordained, and specially created to be the Spouse of the Eternal Love; the True Mother of the Son of God. Let every creature be silent and tremble.

In spite of you, impious Nestorius, Mary is the True Mother of God; she conceived Him by the operation of the Holy Ghost; she formed His body with her blood; she clothed God with her own flesh. *(S. Anselm, de excell. Virg., c. 4).* She bore Him nine months in her most pure womb; she brought Him forth without stain of her virginal purity; she nursed and brought Him up, and He was subject to her, He obeyed her, loved her, and honored her, His True Mother. She may well say to the God made man, Thy

Flesh is my flesh, Thy Blood is my blood; I gave it to Thee when I conceived Thee, when I nursed Thee.

The Flesh of Jesus, says St. Augustine, is the flesh of Mary; and although it was exalted by the glory of the Resurrection, it still remained the same as He had received from Mary. With reason was it said by Denis the Carthusian, that, after the hypostatic union, there is none so close as that of God with His Mother. *(Lib. 2, de laud. Virg.).* Wherefore Saint Peter Damian had no difficulty to say that Christ was one and the same thing with Mary. *(Serm. de Assump. In prim. Serm. de Nat.).*

This is a nobility that surpasses all human and angelic thought; nobility joined to such dignity, that it exceeds all greater highness which can be said or imagined after God; a dignity so exalted, so sublime, that it is a *supreme* union with an infinite Person. *(S. T. I, q. 25, a. 6).* Next to the being of God, says Albertus Magnus, comes that of the Mother of God; and she could not be more united to God without becoming God *(Sup. Missus, c. 180);* and she alone has limited the omnipotence of God, who can make a greater Heaven, a greater earth, a greater world, but cannot make a being greater than the Mother of God. *(S. Bon. in Spec. B. V. M., c. 8).* Nothing can be equal to thee, O Great Lady, says Saint Anselm, for all that is, is either above thee or below thee: above thee is God only, below thee is all that is not God. *(S. Anselm apud, Pelbar. Stel., p. 3, c. 2).*

Now, indeed, I no longer wonder that Saint Denis the Areopagite, at the first sight of this Great Lady, although still clothed with mortal flesh, would have fallen at her feet to adore her as God, had he not been withheld by faith, as he himself testifies. *(Nieremb. Trop. Mar., l. 5, c. 2. Boz., l. 9, c. 9. Locr., l. 3, c. 1.*

Revil. in Paternica apud. Sogneri. Devot. Mariae, p. 1, c. 4). The Apostles and the first Christians were right to erect magnificent temples to her while still living, as did Saint James in Caesaraugusta, Saint John in Asia, Saint Peter in Rome, the disciples of the Prophet Elias upon Mount Carmel, Saint Martha in Marseilles, the holy Magi in Cranagor, and Queen Candace in Ethiopia. But why talk of the Apostles and the first Christians, since even the blind Gentiles, both before and after the birth of so great a Lady, paid her, in their darkness, divine honors?

All the ten Sibyls have told us magnificent things of the Great Virgin, in terms so precise, so proper, that some even called her by her name of Mary. Cedrenus makes mention of a temple dedicated to her by the Argonauts, which temple, afterwards desecrated, was under Zeno restored to her worship. The Egyptians almost everywhere represented her with an infant lying in a manger before her. The famous Druids, priests in Gaul, dedicated to her a temple in Chartres, with the title *Virgini parituroe,* to the Virgin that is to bring forth a child, 100 years before the coming of Christ, and represented her with a statue of such miraculous power, that it restored life to the son of Melancariaccus, a lord of high rank; and Priscus, king of that country, publicly subjected his whole kingdom to her. So also, since the coming of Christ, there is mention of a temple dedicated to her in Calcutta, of one in Coulon, of one in the Canaries, and of a most sumptuous one among the Chinese. Various images of the Virgin are also found in China. Thus these nations, giving homage to the Virgin Mother, by a particular disposition honored Mary, the Mother of God.

Much more reason, then, has the Holy Church, enlightened and directed by God, to prescribe, ordain, and promote all those means of honoring her, which we see practiced, at the present day, throughout Christendom. If the great sacrifice of the Mass is offered to God, commemoration is made of His Great Mother. If the sacred choirs sing the praises of God in the divine offices, after God they invoke His Mother. One day of the week is consecrated to her special worship, other days throughout the year are set apart for the celebration of her feasts. The faithful are invited by the public sound of the bells to salute her three times a day. There is no city or village where she has not a church, and there is no church where she has not altars. How many religious orders have been instituted to promote her glory! How many confraternities have been erected under her patronage! How many congregations of youth, of citizens, of nobles, at each festival, sound her praises! How many processions are formed to carry her holy relics or images! And how many crowned heads have yielded their shoulders to the honorable burden! How many long and difficult pilgrimages are undertaken for the purpose of visiting her celebrated sanctuaries! To the end of the world, men of genius shall not cease to study new ways to honor her, nor pens cease to write her praises, nor tongues to preach her greatness, nor pencils to draw her image. All tongues and all nations honor her. As many creatures serve the Virgin, says Saint Bernardine of Sienna, as serve God. *(Tom. 1, Serm. 6, a. 8, c. 6).* To her, and to her alone, is prescribed and belongs the special homage, granted to no other, which is called Hyperdulia, by which we acknowledge and venerate her as the True Mother of God and Queen of the Universe. Such is the will of God, says Saint Bernard. And why not, since He Himself has set the example? Christ so honored His Great

Mother that, not content with yielding her the dominion over all His possessions, He gave her authority over His own person, with the power to command Him; He obeyed her and was subject to her. Mary had God subject to her. *(S. Bonav. Spec. Virg., c. 8).* Can more be said? Can there be any more sublime honor, elevation, and dignity?

If a prince is esteemed great in proportion to the greatness of the subjects who render him obedience, what shall we say of the Great Virgin whom God Himself obeyed? There is a miracle on both sides, says Saint Bernard: that God should obey a woman—humility without example; and that a woman should command God—sublimity without equal. *(Serm. 2, super. Missus est.)* Nor does He cease now to honor and obey her, although, having laid aside the form and humiliation of a servant, He sits gloriously in the majesty of His throne; it is true, Mary does not now command, but she prays, and her prayers being a mother's prayers, are so powerful that they have almost the force of commands. She approaches to that golden altar of human reconciliation—not only praying, but commanding—a Lady, not a servant, says Saint Peter Damian. *(Serm. 2, de Nat. B. V.).* "Honor, O daughter," said Jesus Himself to Saint Margaret of Cortona; "honor My Mother, of whose beauty and greatness neither the world nor the Scripture has spoken fully."

Saint Gertrude once having devoutly saluted and praised Mary, Jesus, bowing His head and thanking her, said, "I will repay you in proper time, according to the royal magnificence of My liberality, that honor which in My person you have shown My Most Sweet Mother." *(Insin. Div. Piet. S. Gertr., 1. 3, c. 19).* At that time, Saint Gertrude, having prayed Our Lord to deign to supply her defect in honoring and praising His Most Holy Mother, saw the Son of God most reverently rise and proceed till He came before His Mother, and salute her most reverently, by inclining His head, and even bending His knees before her. (*Ibid.*)

O immense dignity, O incomprehensible greatness of the Mother of God, to whom even God humbles Himself! What more can be said? "That Thou mightest fulfill Thy decree, O Lord," I will say with Saint Methodius, "and mightest in this surpass others, Thou hast bestowed all grace and honor on Thy Mother." And what shall we now say of that most sublime position of Queen and Empress of the World, to which He has raised her in Heaven? So great is the elevation of this incomprehensible dignity, that it is beyond the reach of human thought. We may say with Andrew of Crete, that she occupies the highest rank in Heaven under God. (*Orat. de Dorm. Deip.*). But that is still too little: So high is her throne where she sits in queenly majesty that she is placed on the right hand of God. (*S. Ildefons. Serm. 1, de Assumpt.*). She is the absolute Queen of that Great Monarchy, of which her Son is King. She is the Depository of all His Treasures, of all His power, and of His supreme authority. "He that is mighty hath done great things to thee," exclaims Saint Peter Damian, addressing Mary. (*Serm. de Assumpt.*). "And all power is given thee in Heaven and on earth." She is in Heaven the Queen of Angels and of Saints, and on earth she is the Queen of Kings. (*Rob. Abb.*).

And not only is the glory of Mary the greatest after that of Jesus, but we may even say the glory of Mary equals the glory of Jesus Christ Himself, if the great Arnoldus Carnotensis did not fear to say even more, that the glory of the Mother was the same as the glory of the Son. And the reason, says Saint Ildefonsus, why her glory is so great, is that the value and merit of her works is incomparable, and the gifts and graces she has received from God are inestimable; thus also is the glory which she has merited, and to which God has raised her, incomparable and incomprehensible.

In Heaven she constitutes of herself a hierarchy at the right hand of her Son, where, besides the immense glory which she enjoys, wholly immersed in the splendors of the Divinity, fully enjoying that Infinite Good, she has, moreover, all the accidental joys of all the saints and blessed, besides many others that are peculiarly her own, whence she has all the crowns of virgins, doctors, and masters, as Mistress of the Faithful and of the Apostles, of Martyrdom, and particularly of her Divine Maternity; which, being a dignity in its kind infinite, she enjoys for it a most especial crown of glory granted to no other, which is, as it were, the standard of the royal dignity of the Divine Maternity, and of the principality and dominion she enjoys over all creatures. In short, such is her greatness, majesty, glory, and power, in Heaven, on earth, and in Hell, that all nature wonders at it, angels adore it, men fear it, Heaven is astounded, earth trembles at it, and Hell is stricken with fear. *(S. Petr. Dam., Serm. de Annunc.)*.

Behold, Parthenius, how great is the nobility of Mary, as well if we consider her human lineage and generation, as if we regard her intimate union with God, her great dignity of Daughter, Spouse, and True Mother of God, and the immense glory, majesty, and greatness of the most elevated rank she enjoys in Heaven, on earth, and in Hell, above all creatures and above the highest angels, inferior only to God, Queen of Rulers, and Most Powerful Empress of the Universe, before whom not only the most mighty and powerful princes of the earth, but the most proud demons in Hell, and the exalted spirits and powers of paradise, must bend their knees and bow their necks.

O Great Lady, Wonder of Nobility, of Greatness, how I rejoice that God has elevated thee to such great dignity: The Father, to make thee great, employing His infinite power; thy Son, His infinite wisdom; and the Holy Ghost, thy Most Loving Spouse, His infinite goodness! Deservedly do all generations call thee blessed, all tongues praise and bless thee, every knee bends before thee, and all nations adore thee. Deign from the height of the throne, where thou sittest as Queen, to cast upon us thine eyes of mercy, which cannot see without succoring our miseries. Remember that God has made thee so great for the relief of our lowliness; He has made thee so powerful for the support of our weakness; and has placed thee on His right hand that thou mightest reach us thine to help us ascend to Heaven. Protect us, then; help us, relieve us, and make us enjoy the effects of thy greatness and protection, so that we may hereafter enjoy the immense light of thy glory for all eternity.

Seventh Day

You are astounded, Parthenius; you are discouraged and terrified. The great nobility, dignity, and majesty of the Mother of God, which I have placed before you, have doubtless occasioned in you esteem, reverence, and a most profound respect for one so eminent and sublime that there is no greater under God; but, on the other hand, it may have extinguished, or at least cooled, that ardor which you felt towards that amiable object, esteeming yourself altogether unworthy to aspire to its love, or to lift your eyes so high, and you have perhaps even persuaded yourself that one so worthy, so noble, would not deign to cast even a look upon your baseness. But take courage, Parthenius; first of all, call to mind what I have said and made you reflect upon in the two chapters on the happiness and the sweetness of the love of Mary, and consider it certain that Mary never has been, and will not be, one of those proud potentates who join to the highness of their rank and nobility equal fierceness, haughtiness, and disdain.

Such are those proud princes of this world, who deign not to lower one point of their majesty, and woe to him that shall presume to fail, although involuntarily, in even the least part of that respect and reverence which they believe their due. Such was the fate of that poor page who, by the command of Alexander, lost his head, because, having cast himself into the river to regain for the king his laurel crown, he placed it on his head that he might swim back more easily. *(Diod. Sicul.)* So fared that unfortunate general who was condemned to death, by Basil of Macedon, because he had encamped in a position a little higher than the king's. Domitian caused the unconquered Agricola to be strangled, through mere envy, because he had gained a victory over the Britons; and a Roman knight to be killed, because he carried with him a map of the world. *(Tacit. in Agricol).* Laborosoarchod, king of Assyria, condemned to death his principal favorite, to whom he had intended to give his own sister in marriage, merely because in the chase he had promptly dispatched a lion which the king had been unable to kill with several blows.

But far, far from Mary be the thought, the suspicion of such haughtiness. She is as kind, as gentle, and I was almost going to say as humble, as she is great; and I may well say so, for she seems to have carried with her to Heaven a virtue that was so dear to her on earth, to exercise it still in that most sublime position which she now enjoys. Hear me with attention, Parthenius, and you will see if I tell the truth. Affability, benignity, courtesy, and condescension, are among the virtues which draw the heart, attract the will, soften the most cruel natures, and conciliate the most cordial affection and tenderness of the most adverse spirits. But if such amiable virtue is united with nobility and greatness, who can tell the applause it gains and the praises that are given it? How Alexander is magnified by history because he bound the wounded forehead of Lysimachus with his own diadem, and deigned to write to his farrier; Julius Caesar, for the same condescension to his gardener;

Augustus, to his carpenter; Tiberius, to his miller; Pompey, because he went to visit Pandosius without the imperial fasces; Vespasian, because he gave long audiences to his subjects while suffering under a fever; Antiochus, because he visited his sick soldiers in their own dwellings, examining their wounds and applying balsam with his own hands, and binding them with royal bandages; and many others who, in different manners, lowered their dignity to some act of humanity and courtesy.

But what comparison can there ever be between the majesty of these miserable grandees of the earth, already reduced to dust, scattered by the wind, or trodden underfoot by even the vilest men and by every beast that passes over them, with the majesty, with the greatness of that Sovereign Empress of the Universe, who lives and shall live glorious above the highest heads of the seraphim for all ages? And what comparison can there be between the few and slight condescensions of the persons just mentioned, and whatever others history mentions, and the benignity, courtesy, humanity, and condescension, and I had almost said humiliations, which the Mother of God has always used for the past, uses daily, and will use for the future to the end of the world, towards the most vile and miserable on earth, even her enemies, rebels to God and slaves of Satan?

The earth is full, and the world is full of such wonders; all tongues speak of them, all histories relate them, all nations, all generations extol them. I should cover the earth with great volumes, if I should write a part of them; and who can ever know them all? And what pen, or what mind, even though angelic, would be capable or sufficient to relate them? I cannot undertake, Parthenius, to enumerate them, for I should never finish. You already know many of them. You know very well how often she has deigned to console and delight her servants; how often she has called them her children; how often she has hastened to save them in their dangers, to counsel them in their doubts, to console them in their labors and troubles, to provide them even with money in their wants, to burst their toils, to break their chains, to cure their diseases and heal their wounds, to deliver them from the hands of their enemies, to give them health, to preserve them from both temporal and eternal death, to caress and serve them, I will not say as a mother and sister, but as a servant. She differeth nothing from a servant, though she be Mistress of All. I receive, she one day said to Saint Bridget, the prayers of all, now that I sit on the supreme throne of glory, where I retain the same humility as on earth. *(Revelat. 1, 3, c. 25).* And being prayed by Domenica dal Paradiso to smell some flowers she gave her, she made a sensible sign that they pleased her. *(In vita).* The Cistercian monk, Thomas, of whom we have already spoken, desired ardently to see her, and she consoled him with her amiable presence. *(Caesar, lib. 7, Dial. c. 7).* The blessed Alphonsus Rodriguez, of the Society of Jesus, finds himself wearied and covered with perspiration, owing to his age, the difficulty of the way, and the very warm season; this Loving Queen consoles him, comforts him, sustains him, and even wipes the perspiration from his brow. *(In vita).* The monks of Clairvaux work in the field praising Mary, and she accepts and recompenses their praises. *(Spec. Exempl. verb. Laborare, Ex. 7).* A holy priest, most devout to her dolors, and a poor widow, are agonizing on the point of death; she mercifully assists them, and changes their sufferings into delights. *(Cantiprat. lib.*

Apum, apud Sin. cons. 9). A holy bishop of Terento is obliged to restore to his nephew ten golden scudi spent in the relief of the poor; and she gives him the means of satisfying his debt. *(S. Greg. Dial., l. 1, c. 9).*

How true it is that she loves them that love her, and even serves them that serve her, as says Jordan called the Idiot. *(In Pro. Contempl. B. V.).* A poor widow in her agony is driven mad by the violence of her fever, and Mary comes to console her. *(P. Crasset. Dev. a la Vierge, T. 1, Tr. 1, Qu. 11).* St. Dominic retires into the woods to weep, fast, and punish himself for the salvation of the Albigensian heretics, to whom he had that day preached without effect; and, almost fainting away through weakness and suffering, he saw the Virgin Mother unexpectedly appear before him and lovingly address him: "Dominic, my dear son, I, whom thou hast invoked, am ready to help thee." *(B. Alan).* She appeared to Frances of Serrone. While driven one night from her house, Frances was tempted to cast herself from a high rock; Mary drove her from her desperate resolve, and persuaded her to return to Serrone, full of inexpressible consolation. *(In vita).* Mary provided bread every day for blessed Colomba of Milan, of the order of Saint Dominic, when shut up in a house neglected by everyone else.

What more could be asked? A gamester, possessed by the devil, struck furiously with a stone the breast of Mary painted on a canvas attached to a wall, accompanying the blow with horrible blasphemies and injuries, and the wound bled copiously. He was exemplarily and frightfully punished for it by God, who twisted his neck and turned his face to the back, and by human justice he was immediately condemned to death; but the most kind and merciful Mary, unmindful of the grievous affront, by a most wonderful kindness freed him from the death he merited. *(P. Theof. Rainaud. Hagiold gium Lugdunens. Punct. 13).* And to what excesses of benignity and mercy has this Great Queen lowered herself! She has become mother, sister, servant, almoner, shepherdess, not disdaining any office, however low, vile, and abject, for the sake of her servants. Oh, condescension without terms! Oh, excess of humiliation without example! Who will not love thee, O Mary, Furnace of Love, more beautiful than the sun, sweeter than honey, Treasure of Goodness? Thou art amiable to all, to all thou art affable, to all delightful, says Saint Bonaventure. *(Quis enim).*

And what do you say, Parthenius? Do you not feel your heart captivated by so great sweetness, so great amiability? Do you not feel astounded with admiration, to contemplate a personage so noble, so great, so sublime, humbled, so to say, and become degraded in her condescensions, her favors, her affability, her courtesy, her humiliations, and the lowly services which she has exercised, not only towards her lovers and devout friends, but towards her servants and her enemies, the rebels and slaves of Satan? One must have a heart of stone not to be moved, not to feel himself burning and inflamed with love for so amiable an object, in which is found only benignity, sweetness, mercy, meekness, love, and goodness.

To me, O Mary, thou art amiable and always to be desired, for thou art full of goodness, says Saint Denis Carthusian. And what more can you desire, loving and possessing Mary? She is so kind and courteous that she is ever with you, keeps you company in solitude, accompanies you in your journeys, counsels you in doubt, consoles you in affliction, assists you in sickness, defends you from enemies, visible and invisible, encourages you in fear, and protects you from the anger and vengeance of God. If you call her, she answers promptly; if you salute her, she courteously returns your salutation; if you praise her, she kindly thanks you; if you do her any service, she abundantly remunerates you; if you give her your faith and love, she lovingly embraces you, and gives you the most tender proofs of her correspondence and most invincible affection.

But why do I go on describing it? Enough that you have often experienced it; and I may conclude that Mary is a most sweet bait, chosen, prepared, and ordained by God to catch the hearts of men, as He said to Saint Catharine of Sienna. *(In vita S. Cathar., l. 2, c. 3)*. May the whole world know thee; may all men love thee, O Mary!

Eighth Day

THE GREAT POWER OF MOST HOLY MARY

Let histories, Parthenius, extol the power of a Sesostris, Assuerus, Nebuchadnezzar, Alexander, Solimaun, Tamerlane, Charlemagne, Louis, or any other potentate the world has yet seen, or may possess to the end of time: let them boast of their dominions, their states, their kingdoms, and their empires; their riches, their enterprises, their battles, their victories, and their deeds; the display of their luxury, of their power, and of their authority; the enemies they conquered, the cities, provinces, and kingdoms, however savage and barbarous, which they have subjugated or destroyed; what will they say at last? To what conclusion will they come? They will say that for a few years they were great and powerful in a small part of a small point, as the earth is with respect to Heaven, and then *they found they must die,* and see their power be reduced to dust and scattered by the wind. And what was their power? It could not raise itself to Heaven, extend over all the earth, nor descend into the bowels thereof; they could not command the animals, rule the elements, prevent the intemperature of the air, the changes of the seasons or of fortune, nor shield themselves from the many evils that afflict and torment the body, nor ward off the inevitable blow of death.

Mary, yes, Mary is that Most Powerful Empress of

the Whole World, whose power rules in Heaven, extends over the whole earth, and reaches to the bottom of the abyss; she it is that commands the angels and most sublime spirits; is respected and obeyed by nature, and by the elements; is venerated and felt by rational, sensible, and vegetable beings; is formidable and terrible to the demons: her power extends even beyond the confines of life and of time, and makes death its tributary and vassal. Oh, this indeed is power! This is command! Let us examine, Parthenius, and consider that it is all for you—all for your sake.

"All power is given to her in Heaven," says Saint Bernard. *(Serm. sup. Salve Reg.).* Do you doubt it? She is the Lady and Queen of Heaven, and although the blessed, and the saints, virgins, confessors, martyrs, apostles, prophets, and patriarchs, angels, archangels, virtues, powers, principalities, dominations, thrones, cherubim, and seraphim are indeed reigning princes in that great kingdom, yet they are all vassals, subjects, and servants of this Great Queen, whom they all venerate and obey; and she is the Most High Queen, reigning over millions and millions of most sublime and supreme princes. If it be true, and it is most certain, that the more numerous and noble are the subjects, the more glorious and powerful is the prince who rules them and to whom they are subject, think what glory and what power Mary possesses, who presides and reigns over so many princes and principalities. Every one of her heavenly subjects is a prince and ruler so powerful, that all the princes and rulers that are and will be upon the earth are and will be obliged to yield them vassalage and obedience, with their knees and necks bowed down to the earth; and they are so numerous that it would be easier to count the stars of Heaven or the grains of sand upon the seashore than to tell or guess their number, which is known to God alone.

You may now understand what boundless power she has who rules and commands so many most high and powerful princes and sovereigns. And these most sublime spirits it is that serve her and form her court; they are her messengers, and the executors of her every will, in Heaven, on earth, and in the abyss. With reason did Bernardine Bustis, of the order of Saint Francis, say that Mary is the most powerful of all creatures; for although all the saints in Heaven are most powerful with God, on account of their merit, yet she surpasses them all in power, for she is the Mother of the Celestial Emperor, having with Him almost infinite power, for the Glorious Virgin has merited more than all the saints together; whence it follows that she is more powerful than them all with God: hence she says, "In Jerusalem is my power," that is, above all the saints.

But what will you say, Parthenius, if I tell you that not only the saints and angels in Heaven serve and obey Mary, but even God Himself? Perhaps you will say I go too far; yet I may say it, for it is not I that say it, but Saint Bernardine of Sienna. *(Tom. 2, serm. 61).* And what wonder that the Son, although He be God, should obey the Mother, since He even deigned to obey the command of men. Not only on earth did He wish to be subject to Mary *(Erat subditus illi),* but also in Heaven. Yes, even in Heaven He glories that He obeys every wish, every thought, and every desire of hers. "Ask of Me what thou pleasest," Saint Bridget once heard Him say to His Mother, "for thou cannot ask in vain; because thou hast denied Me nothing on earth, I will deny thee nothing in Heaven." *(Lib. revel., c. 4).* Wherefore Saint Anselm speaking to her, says, "That which thou desirest cannot but happen." All shall be done, provided thou desirest it. *(De excell. Virg.).* And Albertus Magnus, speaking in the person of the Virgin, says, "I am to be asked to desire, for if I desire it, it must be done. *(Alb. Magn. ap. P. Rep. grand).*

The reason for the dominion of Mary over her Son is the debt the Son professes to owe the Mother, so that, as says Saint Gregory, archbishop of Nicomedia *(Orat. de excell. Mariae),* doing what she asks or desires, He appears to be paying, as it were, His debt to her; and, therefore, the holy martyr, Saint Methodius, congratulates her, exclaiming: "Rejoice, rejoice, O Mary, who hast thy Son for thy debtor, who gives and lends to all, for we are all debtors to God, but He is debtor to thee" *(Orat. in Hymn Domin),* and consequently she has a special right to dispose of all the gifts of God. *(Suarez. tom. 2, in 3 parte, d, 1, t. 2).* And Saint Anthony holds that God does not grant her a grace when He hears her prayers, but fulfills an indispensable obligation. The prayers of the saints, he says, rest upon the grace of God, not on the law of nature; but the prayer of the Mother of God is at the same time an order and command, for the Son is bound not only to love but also to obey the Mother. Wherefore, it is no wonder that, Saint Peter Damian says, as we have before *(p. 38)* quoted: "She approaches to the golden throne of human reconciliation, not praying but commanding, a Mistress not a servant"; whence it is that the power of the Virgin has no other bounds than the omnipotence of God. For God has so exalted thee, O

Virgin, says Saint Anselm, that He hath made all things possible to thee as to Him; and to this communication of omnipotence that celebrated verse refers:

Quod Deus imperio, tu prece, virgo potes.

("What God commands, thou, Mary, gain'st by prayer.")

Ninth Day

Does it not now seem certain, Parthenius, that Mary is most powerful and omnipotent in Heaven; that she commands not only the angels but God Himself, whose omnipotence is the omnipotence of Mary? Think now what Mary can do on earth, since she is so powerful in Heaven. All power is given her in Heaven and on earth. What prodigies, what wonders, what miracles does that omnipotent arm work every hour and every moment, which she manages according to her own will and pleasure. She is the absolute Mistress of nature, of Heaven, of the elements, of the air, of fire, of the earth, of the water, of vegetable and rational creatures, of health, sickness, life, and death, and what is more, of the very attributes of God; of His justice, His goodness, His mercy, His clemency, His longanimity, and His patience; of the grace, the virtue, the fruits, and the gifts of the Holy Ghost; of beatitude, and of glory—which things she can dispose of to her own good pleasure, and the benefit of her devoted and loving servants.

If she wishes the sun to retard or accelerate his course, she may say much better than Josue, "Move not, O sun, toward Gabaon." (*Jos.* 11:12). If she wishes fire to come down from Heaven and destroy her enemies, or those of her servants, she may, better than Elias, command: "Let fire come down from Heaven and consume thee and thy fifty." (*Kings* 1:10, 12). If she desires the moon or the stars to turn more benignant influence upon the earth, or the air to be discharged of noxious vapors, the winds to be quieted, storms to cease, or the raging sea to be made calm, she has but to wish it, and there comes a great calm. At her pleasure the thunders roll; the waters become solid beneath her feet; the snow-clad meadows bring forth flowers; lilies spring up among thorns; the harvests, scarce peeping forth, are already ripe; the most tasteless waters are changed into wine; food abounds in the most barren wilderness; the earth in its most violent moods becomes firm and immovable as a rock; poisons are converted into antidotes; gardens of flowers spring forth in the most burning furnaces; the fiercest beasts become meek; the most numerous and powerful armies are dispersed; the most formidable enemies are overcome and conquered; the most unconquerable walls and fortresses are dismantled; all nature, Heaven, and earth, are reversed, if she desires it.

What can she not do for the sake of men? What is there impossible, temporal or spiritual, that she does not do for them? The blind see, the deaf hear, the dumb speak, and the lame walk; ulcerated lepers become clean; the dead arise; infidels are converted; those that wander astray are brought back to the road; the obstinate are softened; the most wicked and desperate sinners are justified; graces are multiplied; virtues are infused; gifts are dispensed; merits are increased; souls are sanctified, and paradise is filled with dwellers and with the blessed. What is there that she does not, that she cannot, do, who can do all things?

Do not believe, Parthenius, that these are poetic exaggerations, or rhetorical hyperboles. The rocks and the walls speak; at every step we meet with the wonders, the prodigies, wrought by so great a Lady. "Their sound hath gone forth into all the earth, and their words unto the ends of the world." *(Psalm 18: 5)*. Who can ever recount them, who can enumerate them, though he had the tongue and the understanding of an angel? You cannot be ignorant of them all, you have heard of them; you have read of thousands of them; and I am lost in the consideration of them, and am certain that I should have to live a thousand years were I to relate one of each class. But to give you an example, I will conclude this point with some prodigies of her almost infinite power, which contain a group of portents, and from which you may infer the extent of her power.

And first I wish to make you see how true it is that she is "terrible as an army in battle-array," and that in her "is all the strength of the strong," for the advantage of her friends and those whom she protects and defends. While Spain was occupied by the Moors, after the defeat and death of the unhappy Roderick, the last king of the Goths, many Spaniards sought refuge among the mountains of Asturia, under the direction of their king, Pelagius, who had been captain of the guard of King Vitiges, and was a knight of great valor, but of still greater piety and devotion, to the Great Mother of God, through whose favor he gained many victories over the Moors, the most signal of which was that of 718. He had retired with his small army to a mountain of Asturia, called Aurora, where finding a large cave almost inaccessible by reason of its position, here he intrenched himself with only a thousand of his most courageous soldiers, having sent the remainder of his army to the tops of the mountains to withdraw them from the excursions of the fierce army of Moors.

The Moors, having found out where he was, marched to attack him under the command of their general, Alcamanor, while Pelagius retired with his thousand men within the cave, and there, with their whole heart, they sent up fervent supplications to Heaven, placing themselves under the protection of the Great Virgin Mother. Alcamanor's army being drawn out, he led them thither, and began to beat the door of the cave with a furious shower of stones and rocks, but the same prodigy took place as in the army of the tyrant Eugenius, when opposed to Theodosius. The stones were warded off by an invisible hand, turned back, and stormed the storming enemy, and committed such slaughter among the assaulting Moors that the ground was covered with their dead bodies.

Alcamanor, confounded and terrified at so strange a prodigy, retired with his army, and abandoned his enterprise; but Pelagius, animated by the favor of Mary, and calling on her name, pursued the Moors with such courage and happy success that Alcamanor remained dead upon the field, with 20,000 of his men. The others, betaking themselves to a most precipitate flight, ran some to the river Riva, which horribly swelling and overflowing its bed carried them away with it; a part fled to the mountain, and were buried alive by a terrible earthquake, which threw the mountain from its foundation upon them. And in this manner a thousand Christians, under the protection of the Most Powerful Queen of Armies, who fought for them, remained the conquerors of 80,000 infidels, verifying the words of Scripture, that Mary "is a tower," and that "a thousand shields hang from her, all the armor of the strong."

Let us now see how the power of Mary extends into

the bottomless pit, and how there, more than any-
where else, she exercises her great authority. The
Blessed Virgin, says Saint Bernardine of Sienna *(Serm.
3, de Glor. Nom. Mar.),* rules in Hell. We consider not
now that dominion which she has and continually exercises in Purgatory, where the devout and loving
souls are purged—consoling them, refreshing them,
helping them, and liberating them from that most
painful prison; for of this we shall speak more at
length in another place; but at present we refer only
to that most powerful dominion she has and exercises
in the reign of horror, and over the princes of darkness and the most proud monarch of the damned. Oh,
how terrible she is to these! *(S. Bon. Spec. Virg. c. 3).*
There is no doubt that she is that Most Strong Lady of
whom, even from the first, God Himself foretold that
she should crush the head of the old serpent *(Gen.
3:13)*; and the serpent is certainly no other than the
proud, impious, and cursed Lucifer.

Yes, she has crushed and continues to crush his
head; and howsoever much he may foam, and rage,
and storm, he must remain oppressed, bound, and
crushed under the most strong foot of Mary. "Crushed
and trodden under the feet of Mary, he suffers a
miserable slavery," says Saint Bernardine of Sienna.
He may well call her the *subduer* of the devils, for she
subdues them. *(St. Bern. serm. in sign).* At the name of
Mary, says Thomas a Kempis *(Lib. 4 ad Nov.),* they are
prostrated as by a thunderbolt from Heaven. The evil
spirits fear the Queen of Heaven, and fly at the sound
of her name as from fire. They would rather have
their torments a thousand times increased than hear
her voice, endure her authority, or obey her command. It is then no wonder that at the invocation of
her name they leave the prey which they held secure

in their clutches, as the hawk drops its quarry when struck by the fatal ball, as Mary herself said to her devout servant, Saint Bridget. *(Revel. serm. ang. cap. 20).* Saint Bonaventure says that the devils fly before her face as wax melts before the fire. When they hear her name they tremble, and many are the victories over them which the servants of Mary have gained by the mere invocation of her name. Thus Saint Anthony of Padua, blessed Henry Suso, and thousands and thousands of others have put them to flight. Many devils appeared in the form of wild beasts to a newly-converted Christian of Japan, and tried to frighten him, but he, unmoved, bade them do their worst, as far as they were permitted by God. I have no arms, he said, to defend me from your fury; my only protection is the sweet names of Jesus and Mary. But scarce had he pronounced those powerful names, when the earth opened and swallowed up the beasts before his eyes.

The sight of the largest army does not cause such great fear to a small band of troops, as does the name and patronage of Mary to the infernal powers. Satan flies, says blessed Alain, and Hell trembles, when I say, "Hail Mary." The holy name of Mary is not only terrible to the devils in the mouth of those who love her, but even when pronounced by the most wicked and abandoned sinner, it is even then a thunderbolt which strikes them and drives them from the possession of his soul. A pious writer relates an instance of this, in a young man who had left the sodality of the Blessed Virgin, and given himself up to a sinful life, but was delivered from the clutches of the devil by invoking the name of Mary. *(L'honer. Sodal. Parth., lib. 3, cap. 3).*

Now if such is the effect of the mere name of Mary, what must be the power of that Great Lady herself?

She has broken the power of these wicked demons, chained them, and trodden them underfoot. He who calls on Mary need not fear them, but may laugh at their impotent fury. What is there for us to fear, Parthenius, if Mary will take us under her protection? What may we not promise ourselves? What may we not expect from her who is all-powerful? Who shall harm us? A man thinks himself happy and fortunate when he enjoys the favor and protection of some prince or great man of the world, and yet to what does their power extend? They may give their favorites a little gold, some post of honor, or evanescent dignity; they may, to a certain extent, shield them from the attacks of open enemies, but they cannot enrich them with those treasures which neither rust nor the moth doth consume, nor thieves dig through and steal; nor can they raise their favorites above the envy of the wicked; nor defend them from the snares and plots of their secret and hidden enemies; they cannot even place them where they will not suffer from the injuries of time, from the changes of the seasons, from hurtful animals, from the envy of rivals, from calumny, disgrace, or disease, or from temporal or eternal death, to which they are themselves as much subject as their friends and favorites.

Happy shall we be, Parthenius, if we enjoy the honor of being loved and protected by Mary. She is almost omnipotent in Heaven, where she is venerated and obeyed by the powers and principalities. God Himself obeys her, and glories in communicating to her His omnipotence, and in doing all she wishes Him to do. Who can comprehend with what graces and virtues, and what degrees of glory she enriches us? Her dominion is absolute over the elements, and all creatures, over all life and all nature—what then can hurt us? What can we ever want or desire that she is unable to give us? What calamities, dangers, temptations, afflictions, or enemies can reach or harm us if she covers us with the shield of her powerful patronage?

She is, in fine, the Champion of the Heavenly Powers, the Conqueror of Hell, the Terror of the proud Lucifer and his wicked followers. Neither their snares, nor their deceits, nor their violence, nor their fury can prevail against us; a look, a prayer, an invocation of her most holy name is enough to defend us and put them to flight. Though all Hell should rise up against us we will joyfully sing: "I will not fear thousands of the people surrounding me—Mary is my Light and my Salvation; whom shall I fear? She is the Protector of my Life; of whom shall I be afraid? If armies in camp should stand together against me, my heart shall not fear. If a battle should rise up against me, in this will I be confident, because thou art with me."

Yes, O Great Queen, God has given thee all power in Heaven, and in the abyss, and nothing is impossible to thee; thou canst hold and govern at thy pleasure the almighty arm of God. Take me under thy powerful care and protection, and I shall fear no evil; place me by thy side, and let attack me who will. I say to thee with Saint John Damascen, "I have an invincible hope in thee, O Mother of God, that I shall be saved. With thy assistance, and under thy protection, I will pursue my enemies and boldly attack them."

Tenth Day

THE KNOWLEDGE AND WISDOM
OF MOST HOLY MARY

"He is wise," says Aristotle, "who knows all things." Saint Bonaventure asserts the same thing, when, treating of wisdom in its usual acceptation, he says it is "the general knowledge of things human and divine." *(Centilog. 3 part, sect. 45).* I should not dare decide, Parthenius, whether any man ever attained this wisdom. There have always been men, and sometimes even women, who were esteemed wise and learned. Greece boasted her Homer and Pindar, her Socrates and Plato, her Demosthenes and Aristotle, and hundreds of others, among them the seven famous Wise Men. Rome certainly does not yield to Greece, if it does not surpass it, in this respect. Every age, even our own age, glories in its men learned in every branch of science. But we are short-sighted, Parthenius, and hence it happens that small glow-worms seem to us to be great lanterns, and we mistake ants for elephants. Those very persons whom we regard as the wisest, see and confess their ignorance, and with reason; for they see how few are the things they know, and how numberless, how infinite are those which they have still to learn. Whether, then, Solomon and Adam, into whom was infused wisdom superior to all others, really deserved this title of wise men, I cannot tell you, nor am I going to examine. But that which I can safely say, and with most certain assurance, is, that no creature has ever been, or ever will be, more intelligent and wise than Mary, the Mother of God; and to her alone, with truth and with justice, belongs the title of "Mother of Wisdom," because she alone has arrived at the highest degree of the knowledge of things natural and supernatural, to which it is possible to arrive, and she alone has perfectly availed herself of so profound a knowledge as to obtain with certainty her last end, which is true wisdom.

Among the most pernicious effects which sin caused in our first father, Adam, was ignorance, God depriving him of those lights He had most abundantly infused into him, not only to know the sensible and natural things of this world, but also to raise himself to the knowledge and contemplation of heavenly and supernatural things, and of the supreme and eternal being of God Himself, and of His divine attributes, so that we are darkened, and even blinded, in our intellect, in such manner that we do not even know ourselves. But not so with Mary, who, by a most especial privilege, had no part in the sin of Adam, and, consequently, had no part in its effects; wherefore, as Adam, created in original justice, was at the same time illustrated by the infused light of science and wisdom, so was it most just that so great a privilege should, in a special manner, be enjoyed by her who alone in the whole world was just and holy, and was chosen and predestined to be the Mother of God. Yes, Parthenius, in the first instant of her most pure and Immaculate Conception, Mary had the most perfect use of reason, and an incomprehensible and most perfect knowledge of all natural and supernatural things infused into her by God, in the most sublime degree possible for a pure creature. This is the common opinion of the doctors and fathers of the Church.

Therefore, in that first instant, she knew the supreme essence of God, with all His infinite perfections and attributes, in a most high manner, and with such light and clearness of vision, that although she did not see and know God intuitively and face to face, still she saw and knew Him abstractly, in the most perfect manner in which God manifests Himself to the created intellect. She saw and knew the existence and nature of God, with all His divine attributes and prerogatives; His eternity, infinity, simplicity, and perfections; the immutability, immensity, incomprehensibility, goodness, intellect, wisdom, power, will, love, justice, mercy, providence, and all the other perfections that are found in God. The ineffable mystery of the Most Holy Trinity of the Father, the Son, and the Holy Ghost, distinct among themselves, but not divided, and that all three constitute One Only and True God, one only and most simple essence in three distinct hypostases, was manifested to her; the generation of the Word, the procession of the Holy Ghost, and all that belongs to this admirable mystery. *(S. Anton. P. 4, 41).* She saw and understood the immense goodness of God, who being eternally most blessed in Himself, without having need of anyone, was yet pleased to communicate Himself *ad extra,* and therefore was pleased to create the whole world from nothing, with all the things that are in it, making them sharers of His infinite perfections.

She knew the creation of the angels, their nature, their orders and hierarchies, their place, their motion, their power, their understanding and speech, with all their qualities and perfections; the pride and fall of Lucifer, and of his followers; the eternal pains and chastisement to which they were therefore con-

demned; the place of their punishment; the beatitude
of the angels who remained faithful and submissive to
God; paradise, the most glorious seat of God, and the
blessed country of those most happy spirits, and of all
the elect; the place destined for the eternal punishment of the reprobate, and for the just retribution for
their faults; the creation of man made to the image
and likeness of God; the nature and powers of the rational soul; the disobedience of Adam, his chastisement, the privation of the natural and supernatural
gifts with which God had enriched him, and of the
beatitude to which he was destined; the penalties and
miseries to which he was condemned, with all his
posterity; the causes and the decree of the Incarnation of the second Person of the most Holy Trinity in
the womb of a Most Pure Virgin, the hypostatic union
of the Word with the most holy humanity of Christ;
the grace, the gifts, the virtues, the merits, the life,
preaching, Passion, death, and Resurrection of the
Redeemer; the restoration and the salvation of the
human race; the sacraments and their efficacy; the
Church, the elect, and the reprobate—yes,
Parthenius, she saw and knew you and me, and even
then she loved us, and desired and obtained for us all
that was good.

She had a perfect knowledge of the mystery of the
Incarnation, says Saint Antoninus together with
Albertus Magnus, of her own soul, and of all spirits, of
the Scriptures, of things to be done, and to be
contemplated. She saw the angels, the souls of men,
and the devils, whether they were in this world or in
eternity. She had the most perfect knowledge of the
constituents of the body. She knew the causes, the
production, the effects, nature, substance, qualities,
properties, position, place, motion, and virtues of the

heavens, of the sun, of the moon, stars, planets, fire, air, water, and earth; of the herbs, flowers, and fruits; of the salts, sugars, and minerals; of the birds, fishes, and all animals; their structure and economy, their parts, kinds, species, varieties, and nourishment; also, light, colors, odors, tastes, and whatever else there is in the order of nature, created by God. She was fully informed and instructed of the origin of the world, of the propagation of the human race, of the division of the earth, of the customs, humors, qualities, effects, passions, and religions of all nations. She understood the order, progress, and decline of principalities, kingdoms, and empires; she knew all that happened from the beginning of the world, or will happen at the end of time.

She was specially informed of the vocation of Abraham, of his posterity, of the separation of the chosen people, of the patriarchs, of the prophets, of the kingdoms of Juda and of Israel, of David, and of her other ancestors. She knew the graces granted to her people by God, the prodigies wrought in their favor, the ingratitude and infidelity with which they were returned, the Scriptures, the prophecies, and whatever had happened or was to happen to her nation. In short, she knew all, was ignorant of nothing, as says Albertus Magnus. *(De Laud. Virg. c. 189)*. And in that first instant she was more instructed, more learned, more intelligent, and wise, in every kind of art or science, as well natural as supernatural, human as divine, than not only all the wise and learned men of the earth, but even the angels and most sublime spirits of paradise.

What learning, what wisdom, what knowledge she possessed, Parthenius! Think then, to what degree she arrived, by practical experience, in the 72 years

which she lived, by the reading of so many writings
and prophecies, by so many illustrations, lights, con-
templations, ecstasies, and visions, and by the continual communication, conversation, and intimate
familiarity which she had with the divine wisdom of
her Son, the God made man. Who can tell what great
light and lofty knowledge she thereby obtained? And
if it be true, as is most probable, and many authors
hold, that during her lifetime she had many times the
intuitive vision, face to face, of the Divinity, who can
comprehend how deeply she was immerged in that
Light in which is seen all light? We must confess that
even in this life she was superior in knowledge, in
wisdom, and science to all the blessed spirits who enjoy the beatific vision of God.

Now that, exalted above every human and angelic
understanding, she sees unveiled and face to face the
Divinity in which she is almost absorbed, and which
surrounds and penetrates her with immense light,
what does she not see in that Bright Mirror? All the
most profound secrets communicated to a pure
creature, are open to her. She can almost say that God
has made known to her all His secret mysteries and
judgments. And to contemplate Him in whose light we
see the light, what inaccessible light must He not have
communicated to her whom He has chosen for His
Mother, and with whom He has divided His empire,
constituting her the Queen and Empress of the World.
And if, for the mere governing of a worldly kingdom,
and that not one of the largest, God communicated
such light and wisdom to a Solomon, what wisdom and
light must not God have communicated to the Most
Pure, Most Beloved, and Most Exalted of His
creatures, to His Daughter, Mother, and Spouse, for
the enlightening, ruling, and governing of an entire

world, celestial and terrestrial. She was to be the Mother and Mistress of all nations, of all peoples, of all men; it was then necessary that she should see and know their wants and their necessities, as well temporal as spiritual, their difficulties, their thoughts and desires, their ignorance and their errors, their dangers, and whatever might befall them; and for this, what enlightenment, what foresight, and what wisdom did she not need!

Oh! We lose ourselves, Parthenius, and confess our total blindness when we come, not to comprehend, but to reflect on the prerogatives of so exalted a subject. She is represented clothed with the sun, says Saint Bernard, in confirmation of what we have advanced *(In Serm. Sign. Magn.),* because she has penetrated the most profound abyss of the Divine Wisdom, beyond what it is possible to declare; that as far as the condition of a creature may permit, she may be united to inaccessible light. Yes, exalted Lady, Mother of the Great Wisdom, thy spirit, O Mary, liveth forever. Thou observest all things, thou beholdest all things, and thy sight reaches all.

Eleventh Day

CONTINUATION OF THE SAME SUBJECT

But this wisdom, this science, is not, Parthenius, purely speculative, and therefore vain, idle, and useless, as was that of the ancient wise men, who, with sounding trumpets gave out dogmas and doctrines, and were proud of their wisdom—I had better said, of their ignorance; and then they knew not how to use the light and wisdom which God gave them, to know and adore, serve and love their First Beginning, and to obtain their Last End, nor even to know and teach the truth to their deluded followers. They were blind, senseless, ignorant, and too proud in their wisdom, their learning, and their foolish philosophy.

Mary is the true science, perfect wisdom, which, according to Saint Bonaventure, neglecting not speculation, makes a practical use of her wisdom *(De Don. Sc. c. 2),* and, therefore, even from the first instant of her most pure conception, in which she knew God, her Creator, and the Author of her sanctification and glory, with heroic acts of piety and of religion she adored, loved, and praised Him; she thanked and feared Him with sacrifices of magnificence and of glory, and with acts of so profound humiliation and self-abasement, that, in that first act, she surpassed in efficacy and merit all the saints and blessed, and the very angels themselves, in their most sublime perfection and sanctity. To her first beginning and last end she directed all the thoughts, words, and actions of every moment of her most holy life, even the smallest and most indifferent. And, therefore, she used all her senses, all the members of her most pure body, all the powers of her most innocent soul, all the profound intuitions, illustrations, virtues, graces, and gifts of all the creatures that depended on her will, to serve, love, praise, thank, and glorify her God, and to obtain the reparation and salvation of the whole human race.

Oh! How often she prayed and obtained graces for me, and for you, Parthenius! She taught the apostles, instructed the disciples, counselled the doubtful, strengthened the weak, animated the desponding, converted the infidels, brought back those who had gone astray, corrected errors, rooted out heresies, and as a Most Wise Mistress established the Church committed and recommended to her by her Most Holy Son at His death, and before His glorious Ascension into Heaven. And now that she sees and knows, in God, the wants, general and particular, of this Church, attacked by so many errors and heresies, by so much blindness and ignorance, so many perplexities, doubts, and fears, oh, how she diffuses the rays of her wisdom upon it; how she illuminates and enlightens it; how she discloses the errors, makes known the plots, evils, and sophisms of him who tries to mislead it!

Thou alone, sings the holy Church, thou alone hast destroyed all heresies throughout the whole world. What good advice she gives! "I, wisdom, dwell in counsel, and am present in learned thoughts." (*Prov.* 8:12). She enlightens the Church to prescribe salutary laws, and guide men in the search for true riches, true glory, and true happiness. She has enlightened and brought to the bosom of the Church whole nations and kingdoms in India, in Japan, in Asia, Africa, and

America. "By thee," says Clement of Alexandria *(Homil. contra Nestor),* "every creature detained in the worship of idols has been brought to the knowledge of the truth, and faithful men have been led to the Holy Baptism."

Innumerable are the lights and inspirations which at every hour and every moment she pours upon us, upon all the faithful, but especially those who have recourse to her. Saint Gregory, bishop of Neocesarea, called, on account of the many miracles he wrought, *Thaumaturgus,* was an example of this. Fearing that he might fall into some error of Origen, of which there was then so much danger, especially concerning the Most Holy Trinity, and having recourse to the Mother of Light and of Wisdom, he merited that she should visibly appear to him, in company with Saint John the Evangelist, and fully instruct him in this ineffable mystery. Being thereby enlightened, he immediately formed that rule of faith which he used afterwards in preaching, and left behind him to posterity, that it might be also taught by others. This rule of faith was approved by the Eastern and Western Church, and preserved as a treasure sent from Heaven by the Mother of Wisdom, as Baronius relates: "Thus the Great Virgin fulfilled what her beautiful name signifies, which is interpreted *one who enlightens,* having always shown herself a *Mistress of Religion and Faith,* as was defined by the Abbot Ruperto, a *Teacher of All Nations,* according to Saint Augustine; and perhaps it was for this reason that Richard of Saint Laurence, among other titles, called her the *Mouth of the Church.*" *(Annal. ad an. 238, no. 15).*

But so kind and courteous is she, that she not only communicates her wisdom to those who desire to be instructed in superhuman and celestial knowledge, but even to those who wish to advance in human science. Albert, called the Great, on account of his wonderful wisdom and learning, was of an intellect so dull to apprehend, and of a memory so faithless to retain, that, being unable to bear the shame and confusion he felt in the presence of his classmates, he determined to leave the order of Saint Dominic, whose sacred habit he wore, and would have done so if the Mother of Wisdom had not come to his help in this danger. She appeared to him in a vision, and sweetly reproving him for the resolution he had conceived, promptly offered to open his mind either to human or divine science, as he should prefer. He chose the human and philosophic, perhaps because this was what he then had in hand, and he had not yet studied the bright mysteries of sacred theology. "It shall be granted thee," said the Virgin, "but because thou hast preferred human wisdom to divine, that of Aristotle to that of my Divine Son, know, that in the last years of thy life thou shalt lose all the knowledge thou shalt have acquired, and shalt become as ignorant as thou now art."

So spoke the Virgin, and so it was. He became the oracle of the schools, and the miracle of science; he illustrated by his profound learning the most conspicuous chairs, the most famous universities, and enriched the world with such fruits of his miraculous understanding, that it is said he composed as many as 800 volumes, and he had the singular glory of having had for his scholar the master of theologians and angel of the schools, Saint Thomas of Aquin. What the Blessed Virgin had foretold, happened three years before his death, and that great man, who was the master of intellects and a miracle of wisdom, was in a moment reduced to the simplicity of a child; but full of merit and of divine science, with which the Mother of Wisdom had enriched him, he happily fulfilled his course in the eighty-seventh year of his life. *(Fr. Jer. Plattus, On the Happiness of the Religious State, book 2, c. 33).*

Behold, Parthenius, how great is the wisdom and science of this Great Lady, infused into her by God, increased by continual illustrations from the Divinity, perfected by the communication and intimate familiarity which she had with the divine wisdom of the Word made man for so many years that she lived with Him, and brought to its height in her exaltation to that most luminous throne, near to the splendors of the Divinity: not useless, not idle, but ever acting and operating to the praise, glory, and love of the Sovereign Good, and to the enlightening and salvation of the human race.

Can anything more be said? Can any creature be found more learned, more wise, more enlightened? Any teacher more intelligent and more assiduous in communicating kindly and copiously her lights, to instruct and illuminate the darkness of the world? She well deserves the title, given her by the Holy Church, of "Seat of Wisdom"—because the True Wisdom resides in her, as on Its throne. She is the True Dawn that drives the darkness before her, and is followed by the Sun of Justice. She is the Star of Jacob, to use an expression of Saint Bernard's, whose ray enlightens the world, shines in Heaven, penetrates into Hell, warms the mind, produces virtue, and burns and consumes every vice; the Star of the great stormy sea of this world, which shows us our path, and conducts us to the port of salvation through the midst of waves and tempests.

Let us not, then, turn our eyes from the light of this

Star, if we wish not to be driven astray by storms; if the winds of temptation blow upon us, if we strike against the rocks of tribulation, let us look upon this Star, let us call upon Mary; if the impetuous waves of pride, ambition, detraction, and envy, agitate and toss us about, let us look upon this Star, let us call upon Mary; if anger, or avarice, or the enticements of the senses, place the small and leaking ship of our soul in danger of shipwreck, let us turn our eyes upon this Star, let us call upon Mary; if, troubled by the grievousness and number of our past errors and excesses, confounded by remorse of conscience, terrified by the approaching judgment, we find ourselves already absorbed in an abyss of grief and despair, let us think of Mary, let us invoke Mary.

In dangers, in difficulties, in doubts, in fears, let us turn to this Star, let us think of Mary, let us invoke Mary, let her not be far from our mouth, from our mind, from our heart; and that we may enjoy her patronage, let us not fear to imitate her: following in her steps, we shall not go astray; if we call upon her, we shall not despair of our salvation; thinking of her, we shall not fall into error; if she extends her hand to us, we shall not fall; under her patronage, we shall not fear; and, finally, with her guidance and help, we shall arrive safe and sound at the port of eternal salvation, to which she will happily lead us.

Twelfth Day

"Happy is the husband of a good wife," says the Holy Ghost. (*Ecclus.* 26:1). "A virtuous woman rejoiceth her husband, and shall fulfill the years of his life in peace." (*Ecclus.* 26:2). "He that hath found a good wife hath found a good thing, and shall receive a pleasure from the Lord" (*Prov.* 18:22), "for the grace of her modesty is above gold." (*Prov.* 7:21).

Such expressions are met with at every step in the Scripture, which, in the thirty-first chapter of the book of Proverbs, gives a picture, and most glorious eulogy of such a woman. "The heart of her husband," it says, "trusteth in her, and he shall have no need of spoils. She will render him good, not evil, all the days of her life. She hath sought wool and flax, and hath wrought by the counsel of her hands. She is like the merchant's ship, she bringeth her bread from afar. And she hath risen in the night, and given a prey to her household, and victuals to her maidens. She hath considered a field, and bought it; with the fruit of her hands she hath planted a vineyard. She hath girded her loins with strength, and has strengthened her arm. She hath tasted and seen that her traffic is good; her lamp shall not be put out in the night. She hath put out her hand to strong things, and her fingers have taken hold of the spindle. She hath opened her hand to the needy, and stretched out her hands to the poor. She

75

shall not fear for her house in the cold of snow, for all her domestics are clothed with double garments. She hath made for herself clothing of tapestry, fine linen and purple is her covering. Her husband is honorable in the gates, when he sitteth among the senators of the land. She hath made fine linen and sold it, and delivered a girdle to the Chanaanite. Strength and beauty are her clothing; and she shall laugh in the latter day. She hath opened her mouth to wisdom, and the law of clemency is on her tongue. She hath looked well to the paths of her house, and hath not eaten her bread idle. Her children rose up and called her blessed; her husband, and he praised her. Many daughters have gathered together riches; thou hast surpassed them all. Favor is deceitful, and beauty is vain; the woman that feareth the Lord, she shall be praised. Give her the fruit of her hands, and let her works praise her in the gates." (*Prov.* 31:11-31).

This is the celebrated picture and magnificent eulogy which the Holy Ghost makes of a good and holy woman. But where shall we find such a one, O Parthenius? Far and from the uttermost coasts is the price of her.

There was a time when this miserable earth possessed her, but it knew her not; we must now look for her in Heaven, and there certainly we shall find her, and she is Mary. She is the Virtuous Woman; to her alone belongs this great eulogy, and it is vain to seek for another to whom it may apply. She alone is great, wise, holy, and most perfect, without stain, without shade, without mole, all pure, all beautiful; "One is my dove, my perfect one is but one."

We will, if you please, give Mary's virtues a glance; and let us see, in the first place, what and how great a capital of grace God has bestowed on this Great

Lady, wherewith to traffic; in the second place, how she has managed and multiplied this capital; and, finally, how, by means of this, and of her most rare endowments and inexplicable virtues, she has rendered, and still renders, herself most grateful and amiable, not only to God, but even to men.

Entering upon the discussion of the sanctity of Mary, we enter, Parthenius, upon a boundless ocean, which has not yet been, and never can be, navigated by a human nor even an angelical mind: think, then, whether we can navigate it. But it matters not; we shall be equally blessed, if wrecked and lost on this ocean of graces. It is the common opinion, at the present day, that the Most Holy Virgin, in her sanctification in the womb of Saint Anne, had more grace, more habits of virtue, and more talents, than any saint on earth or seraph in Heaven ever possessed; they even say that these graces and these gifts were greater and higher than those of all the angels, and all the saints that ever have been, or ever will be, taken together. I shall not here enter on the proof of it, for the brevity I have proposed prevents that; but I refer the reader to the works of Suarez *(T. 2, p. 3, Dist. 4, sect. i)*, Segneri *(Dev. Mar. par. i, c. 3, § 4)*, Carthagena *(S. 1, Serm. 31)*, Saint Alphonsus Liguori *(Glories of Mary, vol. 2, Disc. 2, on the Nativity)*, Father Pepe *(Delle grandezze di Gesu e di Maria, t. 3, lez. 136)* and many others cited by them, who have examined the question, *ex professo;* this view was also sustained by the school of Salamanca, and was so pleasing to the Divine Mother that she sent to thank Suarez for having promulgated and vigorously sustained this opinion, as Segneri relates. *(Dev. Mar. p. 1, c. 3, § 5)*.

Now this being supposed, which is a morally certain truth, can you imagine, Parthenius, how great must have been this grace, these endowments, which surpassed, not only those of the highest seraphs, but of all the saints and angels together? "Now that you may in some manner understand this, know," says Father Segneri, "that the angels are so many that the great Saint Denis, instructed by the apostle Paul, writes that not only the individual angels, but the armies of them, surpass all number that our weak minds can conceive; which moved Saint Thomas *(P. 3, q. 50, art. ult.)* to teach that the angels surpass corporeal things in number, as much as the heavens surpass all inferior substances in size and greatness; and, by this account, we must say that the angels are more numerous than the stars in the firmament, than the sands of the sea, or the atoms in the air, and so, in fact, says Suarez. But they are not, therefore, a confused multitude, like the sands and atoms. No, their number and hierarchies are well ordered, one superior to the other in gifts of grace, as in those of nature—as in number, the second is above the first, the third above the second, and the fourth above the third.

Now imagine that in the lowest angel there is one degree of grace, in the second, two, in the third there are three, and so on. And if the angels, as we have said, are without number, how many degrees of grace will Saint Michael the Archangel have, who is regarded as the prince of them all? He certainly must have as many as there are angels below him, and they are innumerable. Now if you conceive the lowest angel not to have one single degree of grace, but to be enriched with thousands and thousands, as we must, if we consider the angelic nature, who can ever understand how many he must have who is the supreme leader of that illustrious and innumerable army?

Now God enriched His future Mother, in the first

moment of her conception, with a treasure incomparably greater. If then, it is true, as is generally believed, that God filled her with more grace than is found divided among all the saints and angels, what an immense treasure He poured into the bosom of this Most Fortunate Creature! "The foundations of this mystical city of God were laid upon the tops of the most lofty mountains of sanctity" *(Psalm 22)* because she began where the other saints finished; and, therefore, "The Lord loves the gates, that is, the commencement of this great fabric of Sion, much more than all the tabernacles, already perfected, of Jacob," because Mary, as says Father La Colombiere *(Serm. 32),* in that instant, was more holy, more pleasing to the eyes of God, and more worthy of His love and grace, than all the predestined together, so that had He been required to make a choice, He would willingly have annihilated the whole of the angels, who are more than 100,000,000,000 (one hundred thousand million) times as numerous as all the men that ever have been, are, or ever will be; He would have left uncreated so many millions of martyrs, confessors, virgins, and penitents, who were to be born to the end of ages, to save this one creature, who then issued from His hands. "She is above all the saints, and above all the angels."

And it was very reasonable that the Lord should distinguish the Queen from the servants, His Spouse and His Mother from His vassals. The great dignity of Mother of God, to which she was chosen and elevated, is an order or hierarchy superior to all that is purely created, and which approaches more nearly the limits of the divinity *(Sum. Theol. 2, 2dae, qu. 103, art. 4, ad 2um),* as says Saint Thomas. It was then quite proper that she who was destined to so great honor

should be also destined, even from the first instant of
her appearance in this world, to a partiality and richness of gifts and graces, that should make her known
and honored as the future Mother of God and Universal Sovereign of every creature; and that even from
the very commencement she should be provided and
furnished with so rich an inheritance and capital, that,
with the traffic and multiplication she would make of
it, she should have rendered herself worthy of so
sublime an honor and dignity.

And oh, how well she trafficked with the great
talent received! "She hath tasted and seen that her
traffic is good; her lamp shall not be put out in the
night." (*Prov.* 31). This Virtuous Woman immediately
saw what a great capital she had received, and how
well it was necessary she should manage it, and
therefore she applied herself to it, and not even in the
night did she extinguish her lamp to repose and cease
from labor.

Catholic doctors have no doubt that she redoubled
at every act the great treasure of grace she had
received. The angels thus advanced in grace during
that short time they were on trial, and shall we deny it
of their Queen? Albertus Magnus says it is a principle
by its very terms self-evident, that a privilege which
was granted to her inferiors could not be denied her.
(*Lib. de B. M. 69, 70, 71*). And why not? She was
preserved from all original guilt; she received immediately the perfect use of reason, and all light from
the Divine Wisdom, to know the Eternal Truth, the
beauty of virtue, the infinite goodness of God, and His
infinite merit to be loved by all—but especially by her
who knew that she was pre-elected and distinguished
with so many gifts and graces. She was free from all
passion, from all earthly tie, from every disordinate

motion, from every distraction, from all allurement of the senses, from every resistance of disorderly passions, rendered impeccable not by nature, but by grace, and enriched with habits of most sublime virtues. And how can you say that she remained idle? Oh, no! Even from that first moment she poured forth her whole soul toward God with all the strength of her spirit, nor did she ever cease, even for a moment while she lived, to unite herself evermore to her Center with acts of love so fervent, that she astonished the seraphim themselves.

What love, O God of Heaven! What a flame must that be which burnt in that heart, small indeed, but dilated with the excess of her great ardor!

Theologians teach that when we work for the love of God, we merit that the charity which is the principle with which we work should increase in us in proportion to the fervor with which we act. For example: If your soul has two degrees of charity, and you make an act of the love of God with all the intensity and force of these two degrees, you acquire two degrees more, and become twice as holy and twice as pleasing to God as you were before this act. If you make a second act with all the fervor of which you are capable after this new increase of charity, your treasure is again doubled, and you become enriched with eight degrees. If you continue to increase in this manner your capital, the third act will bring you to sixteen degrees of sanctity, the fourth to thirty-two, the fifth to sixty-four, and so on.

Mary possessed all the most sublime habits of virtue, and, in particular, charity towards God. She had the most efficacious helps and graces which can be given, she corresponded faithfully to them with acts the most fervent and intense, she did as much as she was able, and never ceased to act with the greatest perfection of charity. Do you not think, then, that at every moment she redoubled her great capital?

In her first act of the love of God she redoubled the precious talent she had received; so that, if we suppose in the first instant she had only a thousand degrees of grace, after the first act she had two thousand, after the second four thousand, after the third eight thousand, after the fourth sixteen thousand. Now multiply thus for all the days of a single year, and let us suppose, although falsely, that each day she made only one act of the love of God. I assure you, arithmetic has not numbers to compute the amount.

Mathematicians teach, as may be seen in Father La Colombiere *(Serm. 31),* that if a merchant trafficking with one cent today, tomorrow should gain two, the next day four, the third day eight, and so from day to day till the sixty-fourth day—they say (and they prove it so clearly that no one can doubt it), that on the sixty-fourth day this merchant will possess $82,982,265,158,000,596.16 (eighty-two quadrillion, nine hundred and eighty-two trillion, two-hundred and sixty-five billion, one hundred and fifty-eight million, five hundred and ninety-six dollars, and sixteen cents); and if he should commence with a dollar instead of a single cent, he would possess at the end of the sixty-four days a sufficient quantity of gold to make sixty massive globes of gold, each one of which should be as large as the whole earth. Well known is the story of the man who, wishing to sell a valuable horse, asked the price, not of the horse, but of the nails in his shoes, with the agreement that the first should cost a single cent, the second should cost two, the third four, and so on to the thirty-second, and it was found the whole sum amounted to $214,748,364 (two hundred and fourteen million, seven hundred and forty-eight thousand, three hundred and sixty-four dollars).

If we take a chess-board, which contains sixty-four squares, and place on the first square a single grain of corn, and on the second two, and so on, redoubling to the end, the sixty-fourth square will require more grain than can be found in the world, because it would require 1,779,190,850 (one billion, seven hundred and seventy-nine million, one hundred and ninety thousand, eight hundred and fifty) ships to carry it, allowing one ship to three thousand bushels.

Now, if we suppose the Blessed Virgin to have received only one degree of grace in her Immaculate Conception, and that she went on increasing this degree only once in a quarter of an hour, in sixty-four quarters, or sixteen hours only, she would have possessed 82,982,165,158,568,796,600 (eighty-two quintillion, nine hundred and eighty-two quadrillion, one hundred and sixty-five trillion, one hundred and fifty-eight billion, five hundred and sixty-eight million, seven hundred and ninety-six thousand, six hundred) degrees of grace. What an immense accumulation of grace she must have had at the end of her life, after the seventy-two years she lived, if we suppose, as is certain, that her capital did not consist of one single degree, but of more graces than were possessed by Saint Michael the Archangel, and all the angels and saints with him, and that she redoubled the talents intrusted to her, not once in a quarter of an hour, but every moment. For she did not perform a single act without deliberation, and even while sleeping did not cease to work internally and to merit, as many learned authors teach. "After which," says Father La Colombiere, "I no longer have any difficulty to understand theologians when they teach that if the Most Holy Virgin, a quarter of an hour after her Immaculate Conception, had presented five hundred degrees of grace to every man that had been born or was to be born, no diminution could have been perceived in what she possessed."

"To this immense and little less than infinite treasure," again says Father Segneri, "add the grace which theologians call *ex opere operato,* and which does not depend on the act and industry of the soul, but is given by God to the soul on account of the merits of Christ. And who can tell what streams of grace the Eternal Word poured into her bosom when she conceived Him, during the nine months she bore Him, when she brought Him forth to the world, when she pressed Him to her bosom and suckled Him; in their familiar conversations, in His most dolorous Passion and death, in which she bore so great a part, and in His glorious Resurrection and Ascension into Heaven; what rich gifts her Divine Spouse, the Holy Ghost, brought her from Heaven on the day of Pentecost; and every time that she received sacramentally the Most Holy Body and Blood of her Son, which, according to the opinion of many doctors and the custom of the ancient faithful, was every day after the Ascension, and thus (to count the number during the twenty-four years she lived after that event) was eight thousand eight hundred times?"

I lose myself, Parthenius, in this abyss of grace; but I am content it should be so, if I may thereby absorb a single drop; and I conclude with Saint Bernardine of Sienna *(Serm. 51),* that the grace and sanctity of the Most Blessed Virgin can be fully understood by God alone.

Thirteenth Day

THE SAME SUBJECT CONTINUED

Let us pass now, Parthenius, to consider how amiable the Most Holy Mary is become by her inexplicable sanctity and perfection, and by the exercise of all the most heroic virtues. It is the doctrine of the angelic Saint Thomas, that when God infuses grace He pours into the soul with it all the virtues, theological and moral, together with the gifts of the Holy Ghost. Now from this you may endeavor to understand in how heroic a degree God infused the virtues into a soul enriched with a treasure of grace so beyond our conception, and how the Holy Ghost poured into the bosom of His Only and Well-beloved Spouse the oceans of His gifts and of His graces, and how she on her part exercised every kind of virtue, and how she availed herself of those gifts and graces.

Who can understand this, except one who has had the most happy fortune to see her, to talk and converse with her? Except the angels in Heaven, who remain wondering, astounded, and overcome? And except God Himself, who has penetrated the secrets of that more than angelic mind, of that most inflamed furnace of her beautiful heart? But this is also an ocean, Parthenius, which the human mind is not able to sound: if we advance too far on it, we are in danger of shipwreck; let us, therefore, stop on the shore, and consider only a few of those great and stupendous virtues which have made her so amiable to men.

What pleasure, what happiness would it be, Parthenius, to meet and associate with a person who, however eminent by nobility, rank, and merit, were equally humble, modest, affable, gentle, meek, kind, and courteous; as liberal, generous, magnificent, and ready to give assistance as he were rich and powerful; full of light, wisdom, and consummate prudence to counsel, instruct, and direct us; most regular and irreproachable in his habits; of tried and uncorrupted innocence; free from all disordered passions, and from all errors; of a mild, pure, disinterested, and sincere heart and disposition; incapable of deceiving, betraying, or deserting us; most loving, pleasing, faithful, merciful, compassionate, and attentive to all our wants; who loved each one of us in particular as sincerely and with as great tenderness of affection as he loved himself, and even more so; in fine, a person who is exempt and free from all defect or imperfection, adorned with all the most beautiful virtues, incapable of disgusting, displeasing, or annoying us even in the least things; but who, on the contrary, would make us happy with every kind of wealth and consolation. This, indeed, would be a paradise upon earth! But how can we hope for it? How can we find it? Yes, Parthenius, we shall find it if we seek it in Mary.

Mary is the only human person whose friendship and love can make us contented and happy. If we consider her natural perfections, she is the most perfect of all creatures, nor is there any being, except God alone, in whom may be found anything greater or more perfect than her soul and its powers, or more beautiful than her body. If, then, we regard her virtues and endowments, what fine order and agreement is in that soul, what solidity of mind, what fullness and tenderness of heart! Were there ever inclinations more regulated, more conformed to reason and to grace? Was there ever found a more mild and yielding disposition?

See how she, the Lady, Mistress, and Empress of the Whole World, abases and humbles herself to the level of dust and ashes. "Behold the handmaid of the Lord," she exclaimed, with the most profound feeling, when she was declared Mother of the Great God. "The Lord hath deigned to cast a look upon the lowness and vileness of his slave"; "because he hath regarded the humility of his handmaid." She respects, venerates, and obeys her husband, Joseph, as her lord; she does not move a step or speak a word without his consent, without his order. She does the same with Saint John the Evangelist, the beloved disciple, after the glorious Ascension of her Son into Heaven, and the same with the other apostles, whom she looked upon as her masters and superiors. And not even now, that she reigns as the Glorious Queen of Heaven, does she disdain to abase, and, so to speak, humble herself, helping and assisting in all their wants her servants and lovers.

What courtesy, benignity, and familiarity she uses with them! She makes no other use of her boundless power and inexhaustible treasures than to protect, assist, and enrich her slaves. Most wise and prudent as she is, she gives us most safe and wholesome advice; she illuminates the darkness of our doubts and our ignorance; she sweetly consoles the troubles of our heart, and directs our steps; and as a most bright star she guides us through this stormy sea to the port of our eternal salvation. "Blessed are thy men and blessed are thy servants, who stand before thee always, and hear thy wisdom." (3 *Kings* 8).

Blessed are they that were worthy to hear her

voice, receive her answers, admire her prudence and wisdom while she lived. "The law of clemency is on her tongue, and grace is poured forth on her lips." What nectar, what heavenly sweetness, what fiery darts of love, were her words! What a tender, simple, sincere, and loving heart, more than that of a mother or a spouse!

Most blessed Joseph, most fortunate spouse of so great a Lady, to thee fell the happy lot to find and enjoy so great a Treasure. Thou alone hast merited to have for an inseparable Companion until death, for a loving and faithful Spouse, her who made thy life happy, and filled thy years with joy and peace. She it was who made thee so great that thou now sittest glorious among the first, or rather the first, among the noblest senators of Heaven. Tell us, we pray thee, a part at least, if thou canst, of that which thou hast heard and admired.

What humility, dependence, obedience, and respect had she not for thee! I know that thou wert confounded and ashamed thereat, and that thou didst sweetly complain to her. What sweetness of speech, what amiability and loftiness of sentiment, what dovelike simplicity, what sincerity, what meekness, what modesty, what retirement, what purity, what innocence, what elevation of mind and heart to God, what resignation, what conformity to the Divine pleasure, what piety, liberality, compassion, and mercy towards the miserable! What heroic virtue is there thou hast not seen and admired in her? And, especially, who can tell the love she bore thee, her constancy, assiduity, and attention to please thee, to help thee, to provide for thee, and to serve thee in all thy least necessities and wants?

What mercy and compassion had she not for thee in

thy labors, thy troubles, thy wants, thy sufferings, journeys, and infirmities! If thou hadst seen—and yet thou knewest it well—with what a sharp sword her heart was pierced, when on her account, yet without any fault of hers, thou wert so troubled and afflicted at her pregnancy! How many sighs, how many tears, how many most ardent prayers she sent up to God for thy consolation and for thy salvation! How many graces, how many gifts, how many favors she obtained from Heaven for thee, so as to render thee the great saint and prince that thou now art in Heaven, a most worthy consort of the Great Empress of the Universe!

In vain, Parthenius, do we labor to describe the wonderful virtues which adorned Our Blessed Lady, who was enriched with an immense treasure of grace even from the first instant of her existence, a treasure afterwards increased and multiplied by her till it was little less than infinite; adorned with all the gems and ornaments, with all the most precious gifts that could be found in the treasury of her Divine and Loving Spouse. We must say with Saint Bernardine, and repeat it a hundred and a thousand times, that God alone knows the beauty of her soul, and that it suffices for us to know that she is a Paradise of Delights; and if we desire to be happy and blessed, not only in the other life but also in this vale of misery and tears, there is no more certain and secure means than the conversation, society, and love of so amiable a Lady. "Her conversation hath no bitterness, nor her company any tediousness, but joy and gladness." (*Wisd.* 8:16).

Let us meet our good fortune, then, the happiness her friendship offers us, the love of so great, so good, so perfect, and so holy a person; and let us say joyfully with the Wise Man, "Her have I loved and sought out from my youth, and have desired to take her for my spouse; and I became a lover of her beauty." "I purposed, therefore, to take her to me to live with me, knowing that she will communicate to me of her good things." (*Wisd.* 8:2, 9).

Fourteenth Day

THE INCOMPARABLE BEAUTY
OF THE BLESSED VIRGIN

Beauty is so powerful a fascination, Parthenius, that it draws to itself not only the admiration, but also the heart, the soul of him who regards and contemplates it; and once the soul is bewitched with this enchantment, its influence can never be forgotten. Well did Carneades call it a kingdom without satellites, for it hath no need to use force or violence, because it gains esteem and obedience from all, and in all places: all render it voluntary servitude and vassalage. Therefore, Saint Dionysius asserts that the beautiful and fair excites love as soon as it is known. *(S. Dionys. apud Cornel. a Lapid. in Ep. 1 Joan, 4, 16)*. Even the Spouse, in the sacred Canticle, prays His beloved to turn her eyes from Him, because they have made Him flee away, and set Him beside Himself for love. (*Cant.* 6:4). If, then, beauty is perfect in its kind, and diminished by no defect, and accompanied by that gift which is rarely joined with it, that is, by virtue, who can ever tell the wonderful effects it produces? History describes to us many women adorned with this beauty, but leaving aside profane writers, let us consider those only of whom the sacred pages speak.

Of Rebecca we read that "she was an exceedingly comely maid and a most beautiful virgin" (*Gen.* 24:16); of Rachel, that she "was well-favored, and of a beautiful countenance"; of Judith we read that "she was exceedingly beautiful; they beheld her face, and their eyes were amazed, for they wondered exceedingly at her beauty; there is not such another woman upon earth, in look, in beauty, and in sense of words." (*Judith* 8:10, 11). Finally, of Esther it is said, "She was exceeding fair, and her incredible beauty made her appear agreeable and amiable in the eyes of all." (*Esther* 2:15). But what is the figure by the side of the figured; the shadow compared to the sun? These were but the shadow, the figure, of the graces, and the beauty of the Most Beautiful, Most Gracious, and Most Amiable of All Women. Mary, and Mary alone, is beautiful above all others: "There are three-score queens, and four-score concubines, and young maidens without number; one is my dove, my perfect one is but one" (*Cant.* 6:7, 8); because the beauty of Mary was perfect in all its parts, she was exempt and free from all defect and imperfection; she was virtuous, holy, enduring, and incorruptible—which are the gifts that should accompany beauty, if it is true beauty. Let us prove it.

Saint Augustine (*Lib.* 22, *civ.* 19) defines beauty of the body to be the proportion and agreement of the parts with a certain sweetness of color, which gives life to the whole. To all this must be united the grace which consists in the proportion of the motion of all the members, corresponding to the five senses of the body; that is, in the figure and the color, which correspond to the sight; in the sweetness of the voice, which corresponds to the hearing; in the equality and delicacy of the parts, which correspond to the touch; in the fragrance of the members, which corresponds to the smell.

Now no one can doubt, Parthenius, that the most holy body of the Virgin Mary was furnished with all these qualities of beauty. "God gave," says the renowned author of the *Mystical City of God (P. 1, l. 1, c. 15, n. 214, 216),* "to that sacred body the natural gifts suited to the singular ends of grace to which she was destined, to form an order above all nature and grace; and as our first parents, Adam and Eve, were furnished by the hand of the Lord with those conditions which belonged to original justice and the state of innocence, and in this rank they were made more perfect than their descendants; so the Divine Omnipotence operated on the most pure body of Mary, but with an operation as much superior and more excellent, and with as much more special grace and providence, as this creature surpassed, not only our first parents, who immediately sinned, but all other creatures both human and angelic; and in our way of understanding, God applied Himself more in forming that single body of His Most Holy Mother, than all the celestial and sublunary orbs, and all that is in them."

With this measure, imagine, if you can, with what proportion and symmetry of parts, with what beauty of color, with what pleasure corresponding to the five senses, God formed that sacred and beautiful body, which was to be the companion and coadjutor of the most beautiful soul, except that of Christ, that ever has proceeded or will proceed from the hands of God; that body, which was to captivate the hearts of men with its comeliness, its amiability, its love; that body, finally, which was to form in its time the body of a God made man, who was "beautiful above the sons of men." And in fact, says Albertus Magnus *(Super Missus est),* as Our Lord Jesus Christ was the most beautiful among the sons of men, so the Blessed Virgin was beautiful and fair above all the daughters of Adam. She had the highest and most perfect degree

of beauty that can be found in a human body, after
that of her Son; and Denis the Carthusian *(Lib. i. art. 2
and 36),* citing the same Albertus Magnus, asserts that
as the humanity of the Redeemer was most beautiful
by its union with the Word, so the Mother was
beautiful as the most closely connected with this
divine union, and that her appearance was illustrated
by a certain splendor, and her virginal flesh gave
forth a most sweet odor.

It is not for us to say with how great and beautiful
gifts God adorned this His Incorruptible Tabernacle,
chosen from eternity. He alone knows this. Richard of
Saint Laurence says: "How great is the beauty of
Mary, He only knows who gave this beauty; it is seen
by the Creator, but is known to no creature. And
because He alone knows it, He only can make its
description and encomium," as when Saint Bridget
heard Him address His Mother: "Thy beauty surpasses the beauty of the angels and of all created
things." *(Lib. Revelat. c. 16).*

After such testimony, all other proof, all other
authority is vain and superfluous. With well grounded
reason does the Holy Church appropriate to this
Beautiful Lady, all the praises and eulogies which the
Holy Ghost makes to His Mystical Spouse in the Canticle, where, part by part and member by member, He
describes her evident beauty, confessing that she has
wounded His heart with one of her eyes, and with one
hair of her neck. *(Cant.* 4:9). I do not now wonder that
the people ran in crowds to see her and to hear her, as
the holy martyr, Ignatius, testifies, writing to Saint
John the Evangelist, and that he so ardently desired
to go to Jerusalem. "I desire to go up to Jerusalem, if
you will permit me, to see the holy faithful who are
there, especially Mary, the Mother of Jesus, who is

said to be admired and loved by all. For what friend of our Faith and of our religion would not be delighted to see and speak to her who brought forth the true God?"

Nor am I surprised that Saint Dionysius the Areopagite, on being presented to her and beholding her, remained amazed and beside himself, he himself most solemnly attesting, calling God twice to witness, that his breath failed him, and he almost fainted, dazzled and oppressed by so great beauty, splendor, fragrance, and majesty, that if his faith had not withheld him, he would have fallen to the ground to adore her as God; and because the account which he gives of it is the most expressive that can be imagined, I will transcribe the whole of it.

"I confess before God," he says, writing to Saint Paul; "I confess before God, my Master, that that which I have seen not only with my mental but even my bodily eyes, surpasses the conception of men; for I beheld the Godlike, excelling the angels in sanctity, the Mother of Our Lord Jesus Christ, whom the goodness of God, and clemency of the Savior, and the glory of the Divine majesty has deigned to show me; for when by John, the prince of the prophets and the evangelists, who, dwelling in the flesh, shines as a sun in the heavens, I was conducted to the Godlike presence of the Holy Virgin, so divine a splendor shone around without me, and more fully illuminated me within; such fragrance of all perfumes abounded, that neither my unhappy body, nor my spirit, could bear the weight of so great and entire happiness. My mind was lost; my spirit failed me, overcome by the glory of such majesty. I call to witness that God who was present in the Virgin, that had not what I had learnt from you taught me otherwise, I should have believed her to be the true God; for it would seem that the blessed could possess no greater glory, than that happiness which I, now unhappy, but then most happy, tasted."

What do you say, Parthenius, to the account Saint Dionysius, an eye-witness, and who had been one of the most celebrated Wise Men of the Areopagus, gives us of the beauty, grace, and majesty of Our Queen? Do not believe, Parthenius, that the beauty of Mary was accompanied by those defects which are scarce separable from our fallen nature; no, do not believe it. Her beauty was most perfect, and was free from all disordered passion, from all defect and imperfection, which might in any way, even in the least degree, render her unpleasing or defective.

The body of the Blessed Virgin had such a complexion as has never been found in any other of the posterity and descendants of Adam, with such harmony and order and proportion, that she never suffered from ache, pain, or any sickness; nor was there ever created a soul so harmonious and moderate in all its affections. However subject she may have been to the sufferings of heat, cold, hunger, thirst, and weariness, to which her Divine Son wished to be subject for love of us, and by which she gained new merit, still they had no power nor strength to tarnish her beauty and comeliness. She was unequalled in beauty; for hers was all pure and holy, surpassing all the beauty that was ever heard of or seen in any human person.

Fifteenth Day

THE SAME SUBJECT CONTINUED

The beauty of creatures is not only united to many defects and imperfections, which render it less pleasing, but for the most part it is joined with many vices and sins which render it abominable to God and man. Beauty is generally accompanied by great pride, vanity, and arrogance. "Thy heart," says Ezechiel, "was lifted up with thy beauty." (*Ezech.* 28:17). "External beauty of the body," says Saint John Chrysostom *(Hom. 20),* "is full of much pride and arrogance." "A fair form makes haughty manners." *(Pontan. i. part).* "Pomp accompanies the fair, and pride follows beauty." *(Ovid. Fast. i).* "A fair woman is a proud creature." *(Menander).* Experience, also, unites to prove the truth of this assertion. Rarely is beauty joined with modesty. "Trusting in thy beauty," says Ezechiel (*Ezech.* 16:15), "thou hast played the harlot." "Seldom do beauty and chastity agree," says Juvenal. "Chastity is ever at war," says Ovid, "with much beauty." In fine, as Ecclesiasticus asserts, it is a difficult thing to find virtue united with beauty. "The token of a good heart, and a good countenance, thou shalt hardly find, and with labor." (*Ecclus.* 13:32).

But far be it from you to imagine the least imperfection in her who is the Fairest among the fair. Her holy body was inclined to every kind of virtue, and free from all material or natural defect which might place the least obstacle to sanctifying grace or to the perfection of nature. Nor could it be otherwise, as is plain if we consider that from it was to be formed the Body of the Savior, all holy and inclined to justice, and the Mother ought not to be dissimilar in habit or inclination. She was, therefore, Most Holy, Most Pure, and Most Humble in her great beauty and exalted glory; her only study and endeavor was to remain hidden from the eyes of men, and to live only to God; to make herself lowly and contemned, in order that she might render herself more beautiful and pleasing in the eyes of God, and purify and elevate the minds of all who were to see her or converse with her; so that her great beauty extinguished all passion in the beholder, and created an intense love of chastity.

"She never inspired anything but respect," says Saint Thomas, "although she was most beautiful." (*Sentent. l. 3, D. 3, Qu. i. A. 2*). Alexander of Hales says the same, and adds that "This was because the virtue of her chastity extinguished all carnal motion in him who beheld her." Saint Bridget likewise asserts that, "As the angels enjoy the beauty of her soul in Heaven, so also the beauty of her body when she was on earth was, to those who saw her, a source of the most useful consolation; because the interior candor, angelical purity, and fire of love which she nourished in her bosom, shone angelically from her countenance." Richard of Saint Laurence says that "The interior candor and fire of love shone exteriorly in the Virgin, and she who possessed angelical purity had also the countenance of an angel."

But who can ever tell, or in any manner express, the beauty which Mary possesses now that she reigns glorious and immortal in Heaven, making even paradise more blessed? The beauty of Mary did not endure for a few years only, like that of all the other children of Adam, which soon languishes and withers like a flower, and terminates in the corruption and deformity of a corpse. No; that Most Holy Tabernacle of the Divinity, that Sacred Ark of the True Testament, was not to be made subject to corruption. The tabernacle and the ark of the Old Testament were made of the incorruptible wood of Setim, though only destined to keep the tables of the law; but those of the New Testament were to hold the Lawgiver, the Author of Immortality.

Immortal, then, was the beauty of this Most Beautiful Empress of the World; for after she had reached the thirty-third year of her age, at which period the human body arrives at its natural perfection, no change or decline was perceived in her; but she remained, as long as she lived, in that same state of perfection, so proportioned and beautiful, that she was a wonder not only to human nature, but even to the angels.

Thus she was always most similar to the Most Holy Humanity of her Divine Son, in the perfection of her body. And although she wished, after the example of her Son, to pass through the tomb, yet that was granted only in order that she might rise again like the sun, more luminous and more beautiful, and be almost immediately clothed with glory. O Parthenius, if only one, even the least glorified of the blessed, be more resplendent than seven most brilliant suns, what shall we say of that body whose glory and beauty surpass and obscure the glory and beauty of all the other glorified bodies; just as the sun, rising above the horizon, obscures the twinkling light of the stars, which formed in the night a most

brilliant spectacle? And such is the beauty of the
Most Holy Virgin in Heaven, that according to the
common opinion of the Doctors, she would suffice to
constitute a paradise by herself alone, and to make
all those spirits and fortunate souls blessed. "It is the
privilege of the glory of Mary," says Saint Bonaventure, "that after God, our greatest happiness is from
her." *(De Laud. Virg.)* "See," said Christ to the
blessed Henry Suso, as we are told by Blozius *(In
Consolat. Pusillan),* "see how the perfect beauty of
My Mother Mary fills all the citizens of Heaven with
joy and pleasure!" What then can we say of this Most
Glorious Virgin, Most Beautiful of Women? "Shall we
say thou art a sun?" says Saint Jerome; "Lo! Thou art
more splendid: shall we call thee a rose? Behold
thou art more beautiful: shall we call thee a lily?
Thou art more pure: cinnamon, balsam, and all sorts
of spices, thou surpassest in fragrance."

But what will thy children say, when, entering
Heaven, they shall behold that resplendent beauty,
and contemplate it in the meridian of its splendor,
with all those infinite augmentations it has received
in Heaven, elevated above all that is there most
luminous and brilliant in glory, softened by the sweet
and tender manner with which thou wilt receive
them to thy loving bosom? With reason, then, did
that fortunate youth, who, after having so greatly
desired and wept that he might behold thee, at last
had the happy lot to see thee for a few moments, exclaim, beside himself with delight: "O My Most
Sweet Lady! This thy beauty is so great, and my
heart is so enamored of it, that till it comes time to
see thee face to face in Heaven, I shall never have
an hour of happiness, nor will anything in this world
ever be able to afford me any consolation. I must

then lead a life of melancholy and unhappiness." And he was fortunate and doubly happy, because he heard this Lady, as loving as she was beautiful, reply and answer him: "Since then you would remain so disconsolate and afflicted without seeing me, come now to contemplate me, and enjoy forever my beauty in Heaven"; and immediately he breathed forth his soul in the arms of her who does not suffer herself to be conquered in contests of love.

What do you say, Parthenius? Is not this a beauty that is to be worshipped? Can there be any comparison between it and any other beauty that has enchanted you upon earth?

Where shall you be able to find beauty that is perfect in all its parts, free from all defect and imperfection of nature? A beauty so holy, so pure, so humble, so benign, so gentle and loving, so lasting, incorruptible, and above all thought, all idea that can be formed of it, that it even constitutes true bliss, a paradise of joy and happiness! How blind and foolish we are to follow after little sparks which disappear in an instant, and shut our eyes to that Most Luminous Sun which enlightens the world and can render us blessed! Let us love, let us love Mary; and her inexplicable beauty will fill our hearts with joy, with content, will make us shut our eyes to all created beauty, which compared with her can excite only horror. Of her, and of no other, spoke the Holy Ghost in Ecclesiasticus, when saying: "The beauty of a woman cheereth the countenance of her husband, and a man desireth nothing more." (*Ecclus*. 36:24).

"Turn," then, "and change your desires; have you been accustomed to look with delight upon worldly beauty? Look now upon the Mother of God." (*Petr. Celleus*). Thee only do we wish to love, O Mary!

Because thou alone art beautiful, or rather art beauty itself. "Thou art all fair," says Hugh of Saint Victor; "thou art fair within, fair without; within in thy heart, without in thy body: within thou art ruddy, without thou art white; red by charity, white through chastity. All that is within thee is fair, and nothing unclean is within thee. In all thou art amiable, in nothing hateful; in all pleasing, in nothing displeasing. Thou art all fair by nature, still fairer by grace, and fairest of all by glory." I will conclude with George, Archbishop of Nicomedia: "O Most Beautiful Beauty of all things! O Mother of God, thou art the most beautiful ornament of all beautiful things!"

Sixteenth Day

THE IMMENSE RICHES OF MARY

I do not believe, Parthenius, that there ever was any earthly thing more wonderful for its richness and wealth than the temple of Solomon. In it were found, as it were, an epitome or compendium of all the riches of nature, art, and grace, and therefore all the treasures that could be desired. The plan was framed by God Himself, and shown to David; you may imagine whether or not it was perfect. David afterwards gave to Solomon, his son, the plans of all the different parts of the building, of the courts, the vestibules, the chambers, the porch, and the "holy of holies." He gave him the order of the divisions of priests and Levites, and the catalogue of the vases, with the quantity of silver and gold that was necessary to make them. He prepared for him the materials, the stones, the marbles, the silver, the gold, and the gems, besides what he had offered to the treasury of the Lord, and that which was contributed voluntarily for the building by the princes of Israel, the heads of the tribes, the principal officers, and by the people; and which besides the jewels, and precious stones, and marble, altogether amounted to five thousand talents and ten thousand drachms of gold, ten thousand of silver, eighteen thousand talents of brass, and one hundred thousand talents of iron.

The gold and silver were equivalent, in our way of counting, to $144,624,219 (one hundred and forty-

103

four million, six hundred and twenty-four thousand, two hundred and nineteen dollars). The brass was equal to one thousand and twenty-six tons and eleven hundredweight, and the iron to five thousand seven hundred and three tons, two and a half hundredweight. All this is without counting what was afterwards added by Solomon himself. One hundred and eighty thousand workmen were employed, under the command of three thousand three hundred officials and superintendents; of these, seventy thousand carried burdens, and eighty thousand hewed stones in the mountain. The floor was of choice marble, and all the interior of the "holy of holies," and of the sanctuary, was covered with thick plates of gold, fastened with nails of gold, each one of which weighed twenty-five ounces.

Besides the great golden altar and table on which were set the loaves of proposition, according to the historian Josephus, "There were ten thousand more that resembled it, but were done after another manner, upon which lay the vials and cups; those of gold were twenty thousand; those of silver were forty thousand. He also made ten thousand candlesticks. . . . The king also made pouring vessels, in number eighty thousand, and a hundred thousand golden vials, and twice as many silver vials. Of golden dishes, in order therein to offer kneaded fine flour at the altar, there were eighty thousand, and twice as many of silver. Of large basins, also, wherein they mixed fine flour with oil, sixty thousand of gold and twice as many of silver. Of the measures like those which Moses called the hin and the assaron (a tenth deal), there were twenty thousand of gold, and twice as many of silver; the golden censers, in which they carried the incense to the altar, were twenty thousand; the other censers, in which they carried fire from the great altar to the little altar within the temple, were fifty thousand." *(Josephus, Antiq. of the Jews, b. 8, chap. 3. 7, 8).*

"He also made a brazen altar, whose length was twenty cubits, and its breadth the same, and its height ten, for the burnt-offering. He also made all its vessels of brass, the pots and the shovels and the basins, and besides these the snuffers and the tongs, and all its other vessels he made of brass, and such brass as was in splendor and beauty like gold." *(Joseph. ib).*

"The sacerdotal garments, which belonged to the high priest, with the long robes, and the oracle and the precious stones, were a thousand. . . . He also made ten thousand sacerdotal garments for every priest . . . also two hundred thousand garments for the singers that were Levites. And two hundred thousand trumpets and forty thousand musical instruments that were made of electrum." *(Joseph. ubi supra).* And who can imagine the prodigious quantity and value of the gifts and of the offerings that were continually made in the temple and Gazophylacium, and which were preserved in the treasury? We cannot conceive, Parthenius, the richness of such a work, destined to the worship of God, and the dispensation of all those graces God had determined to dispense in that place, consecrated to Him. If you are curious to be enlightened thereupon, read the Scripture, Calmet, and Josephus the Jew.

But this temple, finally, which kept only the tables of the law, was only a figure of the Living Temple of God, Holy Mary, who was to contain the very Author of Grace. God Himself not only formed the plan and design of this Great Temple, but He built it Himself. "Wisdom hath built herself a house." *(Prov.* 9:1). Think whether He built a grand one, and with what immense riches and glory He endowed and embellished it. He placed in it the treasures of all the goods and riches that are called of nature, of fortune, and of grace, not only in order to make it grand and magnificent in itself, but to enrich and make us also happy in it and by it.

It was then, Parthenius, the wisdom and omnipotence of God that designed it, and built it for Himself, for His own dwelling, for His house, for His rest, and for His delight; "He built Him a house." A most intelligent, wise, rich, and powerful Architect builds Himself a house, and builds it for His glory, for His repose, for His delight; and who can ever understand with what magnificence and what vastness, with what good order and taste, with what beauty and richness, He would build it? Imagine and persuade yourself that He must fill and furnish it with immense wealth and riches, and that He collected and gathered there all the treasures and goods that could be found in the world; that He collected and united in this, His most beautiful house, nobility, beauty, grace, understanding, and most perfect harmony of all and each of the parts, which compose both the material and the spiritual: sanctity, and immortal life, and every kind of natural wealth. Then those goods which are commonly called of fortune, as glory, dignity, esteem, greatness, riches, gems, treasures—all these He showered into her bosom, and made her the general receptacle of them all. Then as to the goods of grace, it suffices to say, that the Author of Grace was to dwell there, as on His seat, His throne, whence to dispense them copiously to whoever desires and asks them, and therefore she was truly called "full of grace."

We have already seen, Parthenius, in the preceding

chapter, with what nobility, beauty, and most perfect organic composition, with what enlightened and quick powers, with what a most amiable disposition God furnished the holy soul and body of Mary, even from the first instant of her Immaculate Conception; to what height and sublimity of rank, majesty, and greatness He raised her; what power and dominion in Heaven, on earth, and in Hell He fully communicated to her, constituting her the Universal Queen and Mistress of the whole world; what an immense capital of gifts and graces He poured into her bosom, even from the first moment, and how she trafficked and multiplied it almost infinitely, at every instant of her life. Now doubt, if you can, that she is most rich in every sort of riches of nature, of fortune, and of grace. She is filled and laden with all good, with all temporal and spiritual riches. Well did the Abbot of Celles call her "the Treasure of the Lord, and Treasurer of His Graces." *(Prol. cont. Virg., c. 1)*. Saint Peter Damian called her "Treasurer of Divine Grace"; Albertus Magnus, "the Treasurer of Jesus Christ"; and a Grecian doctor, cited by Petavius, "the Receptacle of All Grace."

But this is not a hidden treasure, a treasure shut and locked up, and only available to enrich the possessor; it is a public treasure, open to all, and ready to pour all manner of wealth into the bosom of him who applies to it. "Mary is a Treasure because the Lord has placed all the gifts of grace in her as in Gazophylacium, and from this Treasure He has bestowed large pensions on His soldiers and laborers." *(De Laud. Virg., l. 4)*. And therefore Mary is not only filled with grace for herself, but is also heaped up and overflowing for us. In the book of Proverbs she glories that she is full and overflowing with wealth only to enrich her faithful and devout servants. "With me are riches, glorious riches . . . that I may enrich them that love me, and may fill their treasures." (*Prov.* 8:18, 21). Blessed, then, is he who loves her, Parthenius, he who seeks her, and who finds her, because with her he finds all that is good; "All good things," he may say, "have come to me together with her." (*Wisd.* 8:11).

If you find the Virgin, says Jordan the Idiot, you find all that is good. *(Jordan in proem. Contempl. B. V.).* And why not? God has placed in Mary the fullness of all gifts, says Saint Bernard, that if we find any grace, salvation, or hope, we may be sure that it has flowed from her. She is Our Life in the Integrity of Virtue, our Sweetness and Our Hope, the Light of the Blind, the Glory of the Just, the Mercy of Sinners, the Reparation of the Desperate, the Health of the Weak, the Salvation of the World, the Mirror of Chastity. *(Serm. in Nat.).* "Whoever," she says by the mouth of Saint Peter Damian, "desires the cure of his diseases, thirsts for the extirpation of the vicious affections of his soul, the remission of his sins, and the eternal rest of the kingdom of Heaven, let him approach me with faith, and from the fullness of my grace I will abundantly enrich him."

The reason for this is plain; for as we receive all from God, and cannot have anything, however small, which comes not from Him and is not His gift, so He wishes that all should pass through the hands of Mary His Mother. The expression is not mine, it is that of the great Abbot of Clairvaux. God wishes us to have nothing, says he, which does not pass through the hands of Mary. And he repeats and confirms it at every step. "He wishes us to have all through Mary." *(De Aquaeduct).* "Being about to redeem the human race, He bestowed the whole price on Mary, because God thus wished to honor the Divine Mother." *(T. 3. Serm. de Virg.).* Saint Bernardine of Sienna, in a sermon for Easter, introduces Christ, who, appearing all glorious to His Most Holy Mother, tells her the reason why He has preserved the marks of His wounds, especially that in the side, that thence, He says to her, "thou mightest draw whatever thou desirest, and dispense it to thy children." "All the good," says the devout Saint Ildefonsus to her, "which the Supreme Majesty has decreed to do to men, He has determined to put into thy hands; for to thee are committed all the treasures and ornaments of grace." *(Cor. Virg. 18).* No one shall be saved but by thee; no one shall receive the gift of God but by thee.

We must then conclude, Parthenius, that Mary is an Immense and Inexhaustible Treasure, infinitely rich in the goods of nature, of fortune, and of grace, corporal and spiritual, temporal and eternal; because she is the Immense, Infinite, Inexhaustible Treasure of God, of which God has appointed her the Guardian, Dispenser, and Absolute Mistress, and all for us, if we will but profit by it.

What can then be wanting to us if we love Mary? In her and through her we have all things. If we want nobility, we have it in her. If we are defective in the members and senses of the body, in the powers of the soul, she is able to supply the defect, as she did to Saint John Damascen, whose right hand was cut off for defending the honor and worship of her images, and she restored it; as she did to that good priest, whose tongue she replaced in his mouth after it had been cut out by the Albigensian heretics, while the priest was celebrating Mass in her honor on Saturday; as she did to Albertus Magnus, to whom she gave understanding to become such a prodigy of learning that he is known to the whole world, although before he was of a most obtuse and dull mind, incapable of understanding any science; as she has always done, as she does yet daily, and will never cease to do, to the end of the world, with the blind, deaf, dumb, with the lame, and those suffering from every sort of misery and natural defect in the world; and she has even done so to the dead, to whom she has so often restored the natural life they had lost.

If we are cast down and oppressed by dishonor, poverty, and misery, and deprived of the goods of fortune, she can easily free us from all infamy and dishonor, and make us even glorious and honored; she can provide for us, enrich us, and make us happy with every good fortune; as Saint Gregory *(Dialog., lib. i)* relates, and we have said in another place, this she did to the holy Bishop of Tarentum, who, having given ten doubloons which belonged to his nephew in alms to the poor, his nephew became angry and demanded them back, whereupon the bishop, in his trouble, turning to his Heavenly Treasurer, was by her provided with money, to his own great delight, and no less to the confusion of his niggardly nephew. Finally, if we need the riches of grace, who can better and more abundantly furnish us with them than she who is full of grace and is the Mother of Grace? Woe unto us, and the whole world, if there were not this Treasurer of Grace, as well to preserve the just in grace as to make sinners regain it; to shower down upon the earth gifts from Heaven, as well as to raise the world, on an immense sea of of grace, to Heaven and to glory. It suffices to say, with St. Germain, that no one receives the gift of God but through her *(Serm.* 61, t. 1, q. 8); and with St. Bernard, that no creature ever obtained any grace from God except through the dispensation of this Kind Mother.

"O Root of All Good!" exclaimed Crisippus of Jerusalem; "inexhaustible Mine of All Treasurers, who is richer than thou? Who can enrich and make us happy better than thou? It is enough if thou wishest, or rather it is enough if even we wish it, and have recourse to thee—we shall abound in all good, in all riches. Suffer not thyself to grow weary, O Lady! Let not our inactivity, our sloth, or our ingratitude keep thee back. Pour, oh! Pour upon us thy treasures; thy glory will be still greater in benefiting and enriching one who hardly asks it, who does not merit it, and returns it with ingratitude. Enrich us especially with those gifts of grace that may render us pleasing to God, pleasing to thee, and worthy to come one day to praise and thank thee without end in Heaven."

Seventeenth Day

THE GREAT LIBERALITY
AND BENEFICENCE OF MARY

It would be of little use to us, Parthenius, that Mary is the Treasurer of All Good, that God has poured into her bosom all His riches, that He has constituted her the dispenser of all His gifts and His treasures, as we have seen in the preceding discourse, if she should remain contented and satisfied with her riches and her happiness, without sharing them with us; and still less if, niggardly and avaricious, she cared not for the cries of the needy, or, tired of their importunity, she should dispense her riches by weight or measure. But blessed be God, most liberal in His gifts, who has not only placed His treasures in the hands of Mary, but has also given her a heart so liberal and so generous, that she immediately opens her ready hands and dispenses her gifts to all who call upon her. She even seeks out the miserable to enrich and make them happy, and the human mind cannot tell how many are her gifts and benefits; the mind of man cannot number them, cannot weigh them, cannot understand them.

Scipio Aemilianus Africanus the second is exalted as a prodigy of magnificence and liberality. Having received the inheritance of Aemilia, the wife of his adoptive grandfather Scipio Africanus the first, consisting of diamonds and precious stones, jewels, gold and silver vases, furniture, coaches, and slaves, he gave them all to his mother, Papiria (some time before divorced by Paulus Aemilius, his father, who led an obscure life, no longer appearing in public), because she had not the means to sustain the splendor of her rank and her birth. This same inheritance again returning to him after the death of his mother, he gave it to his sisters, believing that he would be dishonoring himself and retracting his gifts, if he should take it again. Being obliged, on account of the aforesaid inheritance, to pay in two terms to the two daughters of his adoptive grandfather the half of their dowry, which amounted to fifty thousand dollars, he paid them the whole sum at the expiration of the first term; and being told by Tiberius Gracchus and Scipio Nasica, the husbands of the two sisters, that he had still three years, and might make this payment in three terms, he answered that he might well follow the rigor of such a law in dealing with strangers, but with friends and relations there was need of more simplicity and generosity. Moreover, his father Aemilius dying, he renounced in favor of his brother, Fabius, who was not so rich as he was, the part falling to him, which amounted to more than sixty thousand dollars, and to this same brother he gave fifteen thousand dollars more, to pay for the spectacle of gladiators, with which he wished to honor the memory of Aemilius, their father. *(Polib. apud Rollin, Hist. Carthag., p. 309).*

But it would be the same as painting the sun with charcoal as to attempt to sketch with such small acts the liberality and magnificence of Mary, Our Good and Great Benefactress. We have thus far considered her, Parthenius, as worthy of our love by her amiable qualities and prerogatives, which exceed our understanding; let us now regard those transcending graces which render her so good and so useful to us, and therefore worthy of all our gratitude and love. And if, as Aristotle says, "He that confers a favor, binds as with manacles him who receives it," when we consider how kind and liberal Mary is towards us, do we not find ourselves bound by the chains of her kindness? It must be said that we have no heart, or do not deserve to have one, if we do not yield ourselves to a feeling which finds place even in the breasts of tigers—I mean gratitude.

Mary is, then, most ready and profuse in opening her treasures, dispensing her riches, her gifts, her graces, to him who calls upon her, and has recourse to her in all his wants and necessities. How many humiliations, petitions, memorials, and intercessors; how many months and years are required to gain some favor, some help from men! And you may congratulate yourself if even this suffices, and you be not spurned, without obtaining anything, as but too frequently happens. But not so with Mary. All have most prompt access to her, the noble, the rich and the poor, the just and the sinner, the miserable, afflicted, the weak, the sick, the outcast, contemned, and infamous, the living and the dead. At all times, at every moment, she hears all, receives all, encourages all, grants all petitions, consoles all, and most abundantly distributes to all, her graces, gifts, and benefits. A sigh, a glance, a word, is sufficient, and she immediately comes to meet you, to offer herself to you, and to pour into your bosom all her treasures. "You will find her ever ready to help you," says Richard of Saint Laurence. She has not the heart to keep you waiting, even a moment; burning with the desire to do good to all, she does not delay, and cannot restrain the torrent of her kindness. "Eager to do good, she knows not delay, nor is she a miserly keeper of graces; the Mother of Mercy knows not slow delays, when she is going to pour forth the treasures of her beneficence upon her servants," says Novarinus. *(Umbr. Virg. c. 10. exc. 73).*

The holy evangelist, Saint John, saw her fly to the desert with the wings of an eagle: "And there were given to the woman two wings of a great eagle, that she might fly into the desert." *(Apoc.* 12:14). The flight of the eagle is most swift, and the symbol is well suited to the Mother of Beneficence; because she does not run, but flies, and with a velocity surpassing that of the very seraphim, to the help and assistance of him who calls her in the desert of miseries.

She is the Most Perfect Copy of the Divine Mercy and Benevolence, and, says Novarinus, as God uses wings that He may immediately hasten to help His servants, so Mary also takes wings to fly to our assistance. The Spouse in the Canticle says of her, that her "hands are turned and as of gold, full of hyacinths." *(Cant.* 5:14). And what does this expression mean, if not that having her hands full of graces and riches, spiritual and temporal, she cannot shut them or hold them, but they slip off and fall continually from them as from a turned globe, on which it is impossible to place anything so that it will not slip off? With reason does Innocent III exclaim, "Who ever called upon her and was not heard?" *(In Vit. S. Theoph.),* and B. Eutychiamus, "Who ever begged thy all-powerful assistance, and was left in his misery?" *(Serm. 2, de Assc. Virg.).* No one, certainly, even though we include irrational animals.

Saint Melito relates that in the house of a great lord, most devout to the Virgin, it was the custom when anyone was called, to answer, "Ave Maria." A tame parrot that was kept in the house learnt the salutation and often repeated it. It happened one day that escaping from its cage into the open air, this parrot was caught by a falcon; the poor thing, squeezed in the falcon's talons, cried, "Ave Maria! Ave Maria!" The falcon fell dead on the ground, and the parrot in triumph sang, "Ave Maria! Ave Maria!" St. Bernard says, "Let him keep silent and refuse to magnify thy mercies, O Blessed Virgin, who has called upon thee in his necessities and found thee wanting! Sooner shall the heavens and the earth perish, than Mary refuse her assistance to him who earnestly calls upon her."

And Saint Anselm goes so far as to say that, sometimes, we obtain salvation sooner by calling on the name of Mary than on that of Jesus. *(De Excell. Virg. c. 6).* Not, however, that Mary is more powerful or more liberal than Jesus, who is Our Only Savior, and who alone by His merits has obtained our salvation; but because He is also our Judge, to whom it equally belongs to punish, while the office of Mary is only to have mercy. Besides which, Jesus Himself wishes thus to honor His Mother, who, praying and interceding for us, has all the efficacy and merit of obtaining for us that which our demerits prevent us from gaining for ourselves. Many things, says Nicephorus, are asked of God and are not obtained; many are asked of Mary and are obtained. Not because Mary is more powerful, but because God has determined thus to honor her. *(Ap. P. Pepe. Grand. Mar.).*

But what wonder is it that Mary is most prompt to

do good to him who invokes her, and lovingly and confidently calls upon her, since even when not invoked, not called, she forestalls our wishes, our petitions, and flies to our assistance? She is all eyes for us, and she clearly sees in God our miseries, our wants, our necessities, and having the eyes of a mother, and of the Mother of Mercy, how can she help being moved with compassion, and not hasten to help us, to provide for us, to defend us, to console us?

The eyes of a mother, says Richard of Saint Laurence, are upon her child, that he may not fall, and if he should fall, that she may lift him up. *(Proem. in Cant. 23).* It is not possible for her to see and know our dangers, without kindly reaching forth her hand and flying to help us. She is the first to note and observe the wants of others; she first perceived the want of the wine at the marriage feast of Cana; she well knew what mortification it would prove to the hosts, and that loving heart could not bear to see them unhappy. She therefore anticipated their wants, and did not wait till the wine was all consumed, but turning lovingly to her Son, she merely mentioned their want: "They have no wine," and most sure of being heard, she secretly ordered the servants to fill the water pots with water, which she was confident would be turned into delicious wine.

How true it is that her mercy and liberality prevent our petitions. "She is quicker to help us than we to call upon her, and she anticipates the supplications of the needy." *(Rich. of St. Victor in C. C. 23).* She does not wait to be invoked, but she comes to meet us, prevents and anticipates us, and before we think of calling her, she has already heard us. She places herself before our eyes that they may see her. "She preventeth them that covet her; so that she first showeth herself unto them." (*Wis.* 6). And the reason of this is, that she has more desire to help us than we have to receive her assistance. Nor is this to be wondered at, since she sees our miseries and our wants before we can see them ourselves; she sees them while yet far off, she foresees the consequences, and considers their weight, and at such a sight, can that tender and loving heart remain unmoved? Will she not sympathize with us, and hasten immediately to our assistance? And if Saint Epiphanius called Mary "All Eyes to see our miseries" (*Le Laud. Virg.*), he might equally well have called her "All Hands to alleviate them."

Eighteenth Day

THE SAME SUBJECT CONTINUED

If I could collect and place together before your eyes, before your mind and memory, Parthenius, all the spiritual and temporal benefits, which in all times and ages, in all parts of the world, even the most hidden and inaccessible; to every nation, however barbarous, to every person of every sex and age, however undeserving and ungrateful, have flowed from the most liberal hand of Mary; you would then see her more luminous than the sun, which expands and diffuses its rays, fertilizing and illuminating at the same time all parts of Heaven and of earth, and even penetrating into Hell, and there is no one that can hide himself from its heat. (*Psalms* 18:7). "Oh, how broad," says Saint Bonaventure, "how long, how high, that Great Tree, the Blessed Virgin Mary, extends its branches! How broad towards men, how long to the angels, how high to God." (*Stim. Am. P. v. c. 19*). Which Saint Bernard fully and more clearly explains, saying: "Mary is All to All; her most extensive charity has made debtors of the wise and the ignorant. To all she has opened the breasts of her mercy, that all may be filled out of her abundance; that the captive may receive redemption, the sick health, the sad consolation, the sinner pardon, the just grace, the angels joy, the person of her Son the substance of human flesh, and, finally, the whole Trinity, glory." *(Serm. Sign. Magn.).*

119

Authoritative proofs of this—her most extensive beneficence—are all nations and countries of the world, the temples dedicated to her at all times, and in every corner of the earth, the vows and offerings consecrated to her, the services rendered unto her, and the supplications made to her. The books, histories, and tongues of men, and of all the angels—all acknowledge, praise, thank, and magnify her as the Worker of All Prodigies, Distributor of All Graces, and as the Universal Benefactress. She cannot say what the Emperor Titus often said when he had not been asked and had not granted some favor: "We have lost a day"; because there is not and never will be any day, any hour, any instant, in which Mary has not poured oceans of graces, of benefits upon the earth, upon all men, friends and enemies, living and dead.

"The life of man," to use the words of the great Segneri *(Devotus Mariae, p. 1, c. 3),* "is nothing else than a continual liberality of Mary, who with the frequency and number of her graces and benefits, spiritual and temporal, the greater part hidden, makes herself his Guide unto Salvation." I said the greater part hidden, because in the dark night of this miserable world, we see and know only those benefits which appear to our weak senses, and for the most part such as interest us temporally; because, as we make small account of the spiritual, and have little light to know and discern our true good, which pertains to the spirit; so we have little knowledge of and hold in light esteem those benefits and graces which Heaven daily showers upon our soul. But a time will come, the clear day will appear, in which everyone astounded at his past blindness and ignorance, shall exclaim with joy and gratitude, "This wisdom went before me, and I knew not that she was the mother of them all." (*Wisd.* 7:12).

Each one of us shall say: During my mortal life I did not take a step which this Good Mother of Wisdom did not mark out and regulate with her light; there was no stumbling block which she did not remove, "lest I might dash my foot against a stone"; and yet, fool that I was! I did not know that Mary led me, preserved me, was the Author of All My Good, "and I knew not that she was the mother of them all." We shall then discover that the signal victories which, by the most evident protection of the Virgin, have been gained by Heraclius over the Persians, by Narses over the Goths, by Zemisces over the Bulgarians, by Pelagius over the Arabians, and by the Austrians over the Turkish Lepanto; we shall discover, I say, that all these, and many other most celebrated victories gained in the same manner by the favor of Mary, if compared with the spiritual victories which are more hidden, but more valuable, by which Mary overcomes and subjects the infernal powers, are as a small band in the presence of an innumerable host. We shall discover that the assistance which the faithful have received from her in so many dangers, the restoration to health in so many diseases—although manifested by so many votive offerings hanging from the walls of every one of her temples—are only a few drops of the beneficence of the Virgin Mary, compared with those continual floods of spiritual graces which she quietly pours into our souls. We shall discover, in a word, that there is no part of the Church, however barbarous, which is destitute of the graces of this Great Princess; whilst she knows how to penetrate all hearts, she softens the most hard, waters the most wild, enriches the most sterile; and even the summits of the most lofty mountains, that is, of those who least of all bow down to her with supplication—even these she knows how to assist frequently with her favor, making them pour forth unfailing springs of tears of grief and compunction.

And what shall we say, Parthenius? What *can* we say? We, who, perhaps, most of all, have been benefited by the liberal hand and loving heart of this Great Lady, who has ever been prompt not only to hear our petitions and grant us all graces, but has even prevented our desires, by providing for our wants and necessities, spiritual and temporal, sooner than we could foresee them; who has preserved us from so many dangers, has saved us from so many calamities, has loaded us with so many favors and graces, for the soul and for the body, for time and for eternity. What shall we say? What shall we do for her? O strange to say! The most savage beasts may be softened and tamed by kindness, the most fierce animals have shown themselves grateful to their benefactors, even to recompensing them by doing them faithful service, by freeing them from imminent dangers and from almost present death! Well known is the act of that tigress whose whelps had fallen into a deep hole, but were extracted by a courteous passer-by; the tigress accompanied him faithfully into a most dangerous solitude, defending him always from other wild beasts, and delivering him from a hundred deaths which threatened him. Well known, also, is the story of Androcles, who, having withdrawn from the foot of a lion a thorn which tormented him, and being afterward condemned to be devoured by

wild beasts in the Roman amphitheatre, was recog-
nized and freed from death by the grateful lion;
and a thousand other like examples. And we, more
fierce and more ungrateful than wild beasts, can we
return so many benefits only with ingratitude?

Let us yield, and resolve to correspond to one
who so much loves us and takes such loving care of
us, who binds us to her with so many cords of love
and kindness; and since we can do no more, let us
at least consecrate to her our heart, our love; she
wishes no more, she desires only our gratitude and
correspondence with her favors. Can we give her
less? No! Blessed Lady, My Most Liberal Benefactress, I do not wish that thou shouldst have
reason to lament my ingratitude. I see clearly that it
has been monstrous hitherto, and that nothing less
than thy immense liberality would have borne it.
We have waged war together—thou to load me
with benefits, and I to pay thee with faithlessness
and ingratitude.

Thou hast been unwearied with doing me good,
in the order of nature, and much more in the order
of grace. From how many dangers hast thou
delivered my body! From how many occasions of
sin hast thou withdrawn my soul! Into how many
evils, spiritual and temporal, would I not miserably
have fallen, if thou hadst left me a prey to my passions and inclinations, and hadst thou not taken
away the power of harming me from my enemies,
visible and invisible! How many lights and graces
hast thou not obtained for me from God! How many
times hast thou not withheld the hand of His Divine
Justice, and restrained those thunderbolts which
would most justly have been hurled against me!
There is no number to thy mercies! Let Heaven and

earth, angels, men, and all creatures, praise, bless, and thank thee. I will also praise thee, bless thee, and love thee, O Blessed Lady. From this moment I consecrate to thee my soul, my body, my mind, and my heart, to thank thee and love thee forever.

Nineteenth Day

The life of kindness, Parthenius, is love, and benefits without love are as bodies without a soul; because he who gives benefits only, gives a small part of his goods, but he that loves, and therefore gives benefits, gives his heart, and, consequently, himself. In the last chapter we considered Mary as all liberal and kind towards us; let us now see her love for us; and let us see how those innumerable benefits, which she profusely pours upon us, are animated by an incomparable and incomprehensible love. Let us discuss, in this chapter, the love with which Mary loves us, and if, after knowing in some manner the love she bears us, we do not love her in return, and do not yield ourselves to her love, let us say that we are made of stone or of iron; that either we have no heart in our breast, or else it is harder and fiercer than that of the most barbarous, most cruel beasts, who have sometimes made such a return of love as to die for those that loved them.

But where shall we commence, and how shall we enter upon this sea of love? Here, indeed, is wanted the pen and tongue of a seraph, if even such a spirit could understand and explain in some manner the love of Mary. O Mother of Love, thou, who art also the Mother of Wisdom, thou alone canst enlighten my mind, inflame my heart, that I may know and speak worthy things of thee. Thou seest clearly my blindness, my ignorance, how cold and sluggish I am in loving thee. By that very love, which I know not, yet with which thou lovest me to such excess, drive away my darkness and make me understand, in some manner, how much thou lovest me; and at the same time, with a ray of thy love, inflame, consume my heart, that, like a happy phoenix, all its earthly love being burnt and consumed, it may die and be born again to the most happy life of thy love.

The love with which Mary loves us is invincible. "Thou lovest us," says Saint Peter Damian to her, "thou lovest us with an invincible love." There have been friends who have not hesitated to offer themselves to die for one another. Such were Pylades and Orestes, also Damon and Pythias, one of whom, as Valerius Maximus relates, being condemned to death by Dionysius, tyrant of Syracuse, prayed to be allowed time to arrange his domestic affairs, giving, as a hostage of his return, his friend, who willingly accepted the duty, trusting his life to his friend's fidelity, which was not wanting, as he returned on the day appointed. This so moved the admiration of the tyrant, that, pardoning both of them, he wished to be received as a third party into so true a friendship.

Brothers and sisters ordinarily love each other most tenderly. Parents love their children greatly, sometimes not even hesitating to give their life for them. Wives and husbands also are united by most fervent love, and very many cases are found in which they have contemned and sacrificed their life for the sake of their beloved. The Queen of Ormus, in the Persian Gulf, baptized at Goa in the year 1588, and espoused by D. Antonio de Alzebedo Contigno, a Portuguese, loved him so much that, six months afterwards, when he departed for Ormus, although sure of his fidelity and quick return, she took it so to heart that she died the very day of his departure. *(Histor. Ind., chap. 3).* Edward I, of England, while at Acre, was wounded in the arm by a poisoned arrow; the only remedy the physicians could find was that someone should suck out the infected humor. The affection of the king would not permit this; but he could not prevent the most impassioned love of his wife Eleanor, who, while the king slept, entered his chamber quietly, unbound his wound, and joyfully drank death to free her lord. *(Ling. Hist. Eng. 3, 184).* A hundred and a thousand such cases might I bring forward, which are related in history. If the love of all friends, all brothers and sisters, of all mothers, of all lovers, were united in one single heart, and were to make but one single love; or, rather, if all the men that have been, are, or ever will be, all the blessed, all the angels and seraphim in Heaven, should all unite and love us with a most perfect union of heart and will; still I say, and I shall prove, that all this great furnace of love would be, in comparison with the love with which Mary loves us, as a spark of fire compared to a volcano. This is no hyperbole or enthusiasm of love, no; listen to me, I pray you, and then say if I tell the truth.

The love of our neighbor has no other measure than that of the love of God. The love of God and the love of our neighbor go side by side; they are not two distinct virtues, but one and the same; they are two trunks both coming from the same root; two branches from the same trunk; two twins born together, similar to those two of whom Saint Augustine speaks in the *City of God,* and of whom Albertus Magnus relates that they were precisely alike in mind, disposition, features, complexion, and had always the same affections of joy and of grief, and measured with the same thread the events and term of their equal life; they are, in fine, as says Saint Thomas, two acts of the same habit of virtue, which is charity. Whence it is that in proportion as the love of God advances in us, just so the love of our neighbor increases, because both fall under the same precept. "And this commandment we have from God, that he who loveth God, love also his brother" (1 *John* 4:21), as says Saint John, the great master of this fundamental virtue so greatly inculcated by him to his disciples: "My little children, love one another, for it is the commandment of the Lord; and if you fulfill this, it is sufficient." *(S. Jo. Evang. apud Hieronym. Com. ad Galat. 6).* Hence it is that the greater the love of God in our soul, the greater is the love of our neighbor; and, therefore, the more the saints loved God, the more they loved and suffered for the love of their neighbor, exposing themselves to a thousand dangers, and giving their life for them.

This being so, who does not know that the love of Mary towards God surpasses the love of all men, of all the blessed, and of all the angelic spirits towards Him, more than the sun surpasses a little torch in splendor and light? "Even in this life," says Saint Bonaventure, "the love of Mary surpassed the love of all creatures for her Son" *(S. Bernardinus);* so that Richard of Saint Laurence says the seraphim might have come down from Heaven to learn love in the heart of the Virgin; and so great was the fire of love with which she burned towards God, that, as she said to Sister Maria Crocifissa *(In vita, l. 2, c. 5),* it would have consumed Heaven and earth in an instant.

What, then, must it be now that she is not only close to, but is wholly immersed in the most burning Furnace of the Sacred Trinity! Imagine then, if you can, what must be the intensity of her love for that Divine

Object, now that she so closely contemplates It, and knows and enjoys It more perfectly than all the saints and seraphim in Heaven; with that difference which there is between the sovereign and her vassals, the empress and her subjects, the mistress and her servants. With the golden rod of this measure of love for God, measure the length, breadth, and depth of the love she bears us. As immense, as incomprehensible, and insuperable as is her love of God, equally invincible and above all human thought and understanding is her love for us. If the love of Mary towards God, compared to the love of all creatures united together towards the same God, is as a sun in comparison to a little torch, and even more; say then frankly that her love for us is, beyond comparison, greater than the love with which all creatures united together could love us, as a volcano is beyond comparison greater than a little spark.

To this fundamental and principal cause of the love of Mary for us, which is the love that she bears to God, add many other causes, as that she is our mother, given to us as such by her Son Jesus, in His last agony, when in the person of His disciple, who represented us all, He gave us to her as her children: "Woman, behold thy son." Remembering, then, and reflecting that this was the most important expression of the last will of her Divine Son, that this was His last recommendation, His last remembrance, how can that heart refrain from melting towards us with a most ineffable love? Nature makes not mothers, even among tigers, without implanting in their bosom a tender love towards their offspring; and shall we say that grace makes mothers without inspiring them with love for those it makes their children?

Besides this, our Most Loving Mother knows how

much her Divine Son loves us, who, for love of us, not content with descending from the bosom of the Father, clothed Himself also with our very nature, subjected Himself for our sake to so many humiliations, fatigues, sufferings, and sorrows, and even poured forth His Blood and His life for us by a most painful death. And can she, after such a reflection, remain indifferent towards us? If we hold dear those persons and those things which are dear to those we love, must we not be very dear to Mary, who sees us so loved and valued by Him who is her Heart and her Soul? If she loved us only a little, she would show that she set but small value on the Blood of her Divine Son, which is the Price of our Salvation.

For our sake, also, she is what she is; for our sake she has been chosen from among all women, enriched with so many gifts and graces, adorned with so many privileges; for our sake she has been chosen Mother of God, and raised to such a sublime height of glory. If we did not exist, and if God had not so loved us as to become man for our salvation and redemption, perhaps she would not have been what she is, the Mother of God. Knowing all this, can she, who is gratitude itself, not be pleased with it, and not return us a most intense love?

Yet more. She had, while yet living, a tender heart, naturally inclined and born to love and to feel mercy, pity, and compassion for all; now that her charity has arrived at the highest point which any pure creature can reach, think what a furnace of pity, of charity, and of love burns in that heart, when she sees us suffering from so many miseries, dangers, and enemies.

Finally, not to extend to too great a length, she is Our Dearest Sister, of our lineage and our blood. "Bone of our bones, and flesh of our flesh." We know how tender, how loving is the heart of a sister towards a brother: it sometimes surpasses even the affection and love of a mother; and can so worthy, so affectionate, so holy a Sister not love us most tenderly? Pelbartus *(Stell. Coron., l. 9, par. 2, art 1, p. 188)* asks if the Most Holy Virgin Mary loves mankind more than she loves the angels, and solves this question by the reason and authority of Saint Bonaventure, that as God loves mankind more than the angels, so also does the Most Holy Virgin, His Mother, who conforms most closely to Him and to His most holy will in all things. And among the other reasons he brings forward, is the greater proximity and kindred which we have with God and His Holy Mother, beyond the angels. God did not repair the fall and ruin of the angels, but the salvation of men was so near to His Heart, that He did not refuse to descend from Heaven for them, to live and die a man, that they might not be lost, but saved. God never clothed Himself with the angelic nature, He never took their figure and their substance, He never raised it to such height of grace and of glory that it merited, in the person of God and of the Mother of God, to be venerated by the angels and seraphim with the worship called *latria* and *hyperdulia,* and therefore He never called the angels friends and brothers, but vassals and servants. To us, more fortunate than the angels, He said, "I will not now call you servants ... But I have called you friends." *(John* 15:15). "Go to my brethren." *(Ibid.* 20:17). And therefore Saint Bernard said, "Now Christ and His Most Holy Mother cannot contemn me who am their brother, the same bones and flesh."

What a happiness is ours, Parthenius, to be so united in blood and parentage with God and His Most Holy Mother, and to be therefore loved more than the angels and archangels! We have a God for a brother, and for a sister the Great Mother of God! And here let us stop and reflect on the immense, the incomprehensible love, which Mary, our Most Amiable and Most Loving Sister, bears us. She loves us more than she loves the angels, and yet these are the most sublime, most perfect spirits, supreme princes of her court; inflamed with charity towards her, they render her a ceaseless tribute of service, veneration, praise, gratitude, and love.

They consoled her, rejoiced her, accompanied her, assisted her, served her, and obeyed her, even during her mortal life; and yet she loves us more than she loves them. Can there be any other love more ardent, more tender? Can there be any love which surpasses this? And yet how is such excessive love returned? We have miserably preferred the love of some unworthy creature, who perhaps does not love us, and perchance despises, hates, and ridicules us. But as it is impossible for us to understand the excess of the love which Mary bears us, although we should search to discover its origin, its causes, and its motives, let us at least see if we can succeed in penetrating its effects and qualities, and from these deduce the excess of a love that has no equal. But not to weary you too much, Parthenius, let us keep this subject for the next chapter, in which we may discuss it more at length.

Twentieth Day

THE LOVE OF MARY FOR US
IS KNOWN BY ITS EFFECTS

It seems to me that the qualities and conditions of a true love may principally be reduced to four. The first is, that it be disinterested; the second, that it be efficacious and effective; the third, that it be faithful, constant, and strong; the fourth, finally, that it be tender and affectionate. Now let us see how all these four qualities concur and are in a wonderful manner united in the love which the Mother of Fair Love, Holy Mary, bears us; and not to lose time, let us at once enter upon the subject without preamble.

Love, then, in order that it may be true love of benevolence, must be disinterested, should have no eye to its own utility, profit, and advantage, but only to the utility and advantage of the object beloved. Earthly and human love, for the most part, when not animated by Christian and supernatural charity, is infected with the poison of self-love; in the object beloved, it is his own utility, pleasure, honor, or glory, which man loves. Herod loved his sons Alexander, Aristobulus, and Antipater, but as soon as he found them opposed to his interests he took from them the life he had given them. Cleopatra loved her husband Demetrius Nicanor, king of Syria. Herodias also loved her spouse Philip Herod; but both of them, for the ambition of reigning, abandoned their husbands and married, one her cousin

Antiochus, and the other Herod Antipater, her brother. Such, for the most part, is earthly love; its object and end is almost always its own interest, its own utility and pleasure, and these wanting, love also fails. But not so with the pure love of Mary. She loves us with an immense, unspeakable, invincible love; and this love has no other end than our advantage. From us she wills, she desires, only our good.

And in truth, what is there wanting to her? What have we, miserable creatures, of which she can have any need? She, most rich in all the gifts of nature, of fortune, and of grace; elevated to the most sublime post of greatness and of glory in the whole universe, loved by God above all creatures, venerated by angels and reverenced by the whole court of Heaven, honored with their faces to the ground by all the potentates of the earth, by the whole Church, respected and feared by Hell itself—what need has she of us and of our miseries? And what can we, vile worms of the earth, who have nothing but poverty, misery, and disgrace, give her? What pleasure, what glory can she gain from us, who are only fit to cause her displeasure, disgust, affliction, and grief, if she were capable of it, and who only serve to dishonor so glorious a Mother by our infamous actions? Or rather, she not only sees clearly our poverty, our miseries, our vileness, but she also foresees our ingratitude, our coldness, our infidelity, our perfidy, our evil return of her so great goodness, so great love. Still, she loves us, she has loved us for a long time, and ceases not to love us with an invincible love. Can any love be more pure and disinterested than this? O Parthenius! We are made of stone, we have a heart of brass, if we do not correspond to so great a love.

But not only does Mary not expect, or hope for anything from us, who are altogether incapable of giving it; but she wishes to enrich us, to load us with goods, with pleasures, with joy, and with glory. To this end, to this object, is her love directed. By its effects, she shows us at every moment the efficacy and immensity of her love. Almost before she was born she saw us, knew us, and loved us. She saw and knew, even from that moment, all our sufferings, wants, and miseries, and even from that moment she began to plead with the Divine Mercy for us, and to compassionate our unhappy lot, and demand of God, from the bottom of her tender heart, its prompt remedy.

How much more strongly and effectually did she exclaim than all the patriarchs and prophets: "Oh, that thou wouldst rend the heavens, and wouldst come down." (*Isaiah* 64:1). And she never ceased, never was silent till the heart of God, touched by the groans and sighs of this Amorous Dove, in order to end her mourning, from His bosom sent forth His Divine Word to the earth, to repair our losses and load us with grace. Then it was that Mary received Him into her pure womb, clothed Him with passible and mortal flesh; then He diminished His splendors and made His greatness little, inclined His majesty, and became so full of love and compassion for us, that, after freeing us from infinite evils, He enriched us with most precious gifts. Nor was this done without the knowledge and consent of Our Tender Mother. But after obtaining and hastening so great a good by her fervent longings, she wished to be herself the immediate channel through which it should all flow to us, although she foresaw how much labor, trouble, and suffering it would cost her. "She desired, she sought, and obtained the salvation of all: nay, the salvation of all is through her; wherefore she has been called the Salvation of the World." *(Rich. of St. Vict. in Cant. c. 26).* She gave her consent to the Divine Incarnation in her immaculate womb, and wished to become the Mother of a Son whom she knew she should one day sacrifice for our good in an agony of most awful pains and torments. She conceived Him, she brought Him forth, she suckled Him, nourished Him and supported Him, but always with the view and the strong desire of offering Him one day as a victim of our expiation, a holocaust for our salvation.

And here, Parthenius, we are engulfed in considering, meditating, and understanding, if it be possible, the immense excess of the love of Mary for us, who knew and wished to sacrifice herself, the dearest part of her soul, or rather her whole soul, that by its effects she might give us the most unheard-of proofs of her love. It is most certain, in the opinion of Saint Jerome and other holy Fathers, that Our Blessed Lady, more enlightened than the prophets by the wisdom infused into her by God, by the study of the holy Scriptures, by her continual and incessant communications with the angels and with God, and finally by the prophecy and intimation made her by holy Simeon of her most sorrowful transfixion; it is most certain, I say, that she was fully and clearly instructed, and knew not only in general the life and death of the expected and adored Messiah; but as says Rupert the Abbot, and as the Lord revealed to Saint Theresa, she also knew most distinctly all the fatigues, sweats, sufferings, pains, outrages, contempts, blows, scourges, thorns, nails, the cross, and all the most minute circumstances of the sufferings, both internal and external, which were to accompany through life and in death the Savior of the World.

Mary knew that Our Lord's bitter Passion would pierce the tender and loving heart of that poor Virgin Mother who should conceive and bring Him forth. And even when she was herself chosen to so great an honor, and received the embassy of the angel, and was asked for her consent, without which God wished not to destine and subject her to so prolonged a martyrdom; after a brief but mature reflection, placing before herself the sight of the infinite good which was to flow to us from her consent, which yet would cost her so dearly, she willingly, with that most fortunate *"Fiat,"* consented and offered herself to become Mother of a Son who was to be our Adorable Savior, and whom she was to bring up and nourish, to sacrifice Him afterwards for love of us.

Do not imagine, Parthenius, that this is a pious meditation, an ingenious expression of art. No, no; it is indeed sorrowful, but it is also a most true story. From the hour that she gave her consent to the Divine Incarnation; yes, from that hour she offered herself and her Adorable Offspring to the cruel sacrifice, which continued from that time until it was perfectly consummated on the altar of the cross. At every moment of her life she ratified it, having it ever present with piercing sorrow. She confirmed it more especially in the offering which she made of her Son by a solemn act in the temple. She almost subscribed the mortal sentence in the departing of her Son from her, and in the permission she gave Him to go meet the sacrifice. With reason, then, the holy Fathers apply to her the words used by Saint

Paul, to show the excess of the divine love for men: "Thus God loved the world that He gave His only Son," Saint Bonaventure in particular saying: "Thus Mary loved the world, that she gave her only Son." And in fact, Mary, as Mother, having a special right and dominion over her Son, as have all mothers, according to Saint Thomas, it followed that Jesus, not being guilty of the least fault, could not and ought not to deliver Himself as a public victim, without the special consent of the Mother. And it is in no wise probable that the Eternal Father, who had desired the consent of Mary to make her the natural Mother of that Son, would afterwards have taken Him from her almost by force and violence, and consigned Him to an infinite punishment, without her knowledge and consent. The less so, in that Our Lord's sacrifice was to be an entirely voluntary sacrifice to appease the divine anger, which it never would have been if the blood of Mary, which flowed in the veins of her Son, had been shed against the will of the Mother.

This being supposed and settled as a most certain truth, what a long, continual, and unmerciful martyrdom must not Mary's have been to touch, to handle, to kiss those divine and tender members, which would one day be so barbarously torn and pierced! To hold in her arms a Son the Most Beautiful, the Most Amiable, the Most Loving, the Most Holy of all the children of men, and to know for certain that she must take that Son, that Amiable Son, from her arms and consign Him to the most merciless executioners in the world! "She suffered a long martyrdom," says Rupert the Abbot, "in thought, by the foreknowledge of the Passion of her Son." *(In Cant. c. 4).* What fierce combats had she not to sustain within her soul! How many rebellions of her poor heart her soul! How many rebellions of her poor heart against her heroic resolutions; what resistance, what difficulty, anguish, and death! "She was dying while yet living," says Saint Bonaventure, "suffering a sorrow more cruel than death."

What death could be more merciless, more cruel, than that which she suffered when she had to separate from her Love, her Life, in His last leave-taking, in the departure of Jesus from her to go to death, and in the permission she gave Him? Then, indeed, she felt her heart so cruelly torn, that it required all the power of Omnipotence to keep her alive. As the view of death never made such impression on the soul of Jesus as in the garden, although He had foreseen it, even from the first instant of His life, because that was the place in which it was necessary for Him to give a more express consent to all that His Divine Father had ordained for Him to suffer; so, also, Mary was never so afflicted as when she was obliged to give her Son permission to go forth to meet so many torments and outrages, so cruel and infamous a death. Because then it was necessary that she should solemnly abandon Him to the Divine Justice, and consent to all that He afterwards suffered from the impious cruelty of men, and because then it was all presented to the sight of her soul, in a more vivid manner, by a clearer and more distinct representation than at any other time. She saw Him then all torn, His Blood flowing down, His Body all rent with scourges, His head crowned with thorns, His hands and feet pierced with nails; she already saw Him expiring in convulsions and infamy.

O Parthenius, we should be able to enter the most sweet heart of Mary, and observe the conflict and the havoc which the love of her Son, the love of us, there made! We should there see how greatly she has loved us; how much more than herself, more than her Most Adorable Son, who was the dearest part of her soul, or rather her Soul, her Life, whom she loved more than herself. From this we might comprehend how effectual is her love for us. Behold her placed in this strange, barbarous, inevitable necessity, either to see us perish eternally, condemned to never-ending punishment, or else to consign her Son to the most cruel, most shameful murder that was ever seen in the world. He was her only Son, whose beauty is the object of the love of men, of angels, and of God; whose wisdom is consummate in every manner; whose goodness, innocence, and sanctity are the rule of all perfection; a Son who is also her Father, her Brother, her Spouse, her Creator, her Preserver, her Redeemer, her Sanctifier, her Glorifier—in one word, her God—a Son, finally, in whose humanity as well as divinity, by nature, by grace, by inclination, and by duty, she has wholly and entirely, and without any division, placed all her love; and this Son, this Adorable Son, she must for our love offer and consign to chains, contempt, outrage, to the blows, scourges, and thorns, to dishonor, and to a horrible and infamous death.

O God, what anguish, what horrors she must have suffered! Hadst thou, Most Loving, Most Tender Mother, despite the extreme repugnance of nature and of thy heart, despite the furious and violent assaults of the most tender love of all mothers; hadst thou the heart, the courage, to tear from thy bosom thy Beloved Son and condemn Him to die, to the end that we might not perish? Yes, Parthenius, she had it; and with a constancy that astonished Heaven and moved all nature, she pronounced the unappealable sentence of death against her Innocent, Amiable, and Loving Son, and decided against the love of her Son and of herself, in favor of our love, the great cause that was pending in the tribunal of her large heart. Mary made this great sacrifice because of her great love for God and obedience to the will of God. O charity without bounds! O constancy without example! O victory worthy of the eternal admiration of Heaven and earth!

Yes, despite the internal horror which she felt, despite those struggles which tore her heart, despite those frightful images of infamy, of the cross and of death, which were all presented to her, a horrid spectacle; with insuperable fortitude and magnanimity, she pronounced against her Son an irrevocable sentence which condemned Him to suffer, to die, and to drink that bitter chalice of pain and torment, which He must drain to the last drop for our salvation. And not content with all this, she would be also a witness and, as says Saint Ephraim, the priestess of this bloody sacrifice. *(S. Ephr. Orat. de Laud. Virg.).* She therefore accompanied Him to the altar, stayed by His side, said not a word in His defence, abandoned not herself to tenderness or to weakness; but with a strength of mind, not only beyond our reach, but beyond our conception, she would see Him nailed to the cross, would behold Him raised in the air, agonizing for three hours, and dying—she also being in agony, and dying a death more fierce, more cruel than death itself, offering and every moment renewing the oblation of herself and her Son to the Eternal Father for our salvation. Thus we may call the sufferings of the Mother and the death of the Son only one sacrifice, as their will was but one, and their desire for the salvation of the world was the same. Saint Anselm and Saint Antoninus assert that her mind was so intrepid and resolute, that if executioners had been wanting, she would have crucified with her own hands her Divine Son, if this had been necessary for our salvation, and the Eternal Father had thus willed to take a more complete satisfaction for the injuries we have done Him. Nor can we doubt it; for as Abraham, at the command of God, was ready to sacrifice his son with his own hand, it is certain that Mary would have obeyed more promptly than Abraham, because her faith, her love, and her obedience were greater.

What more can be said—what more could she have done? What greater proof can there be of a love without bounds, without measure? "Greater love than this no man hath, that a man lay down his life for his friends." (*John* 15:13). She gave her life for us, because she gave her only and Beloved Son, who was her only life for which she lived; and she gave also her own soul to a fierce and most painfully prolonged martyrdom, wherefore she is called the "Queen of Martyrs." She would gladly have borne, says Saint Bonaventure, all the torments which her Son suffered, had this been possible; but because the salvation of the human race demanded the oblation of her Son, she yielded thereto. *(P. 1, dis. 43. q. 2)*. She had to do greater violence to herself and suffer much more than if she had sacrificed herself, and she therefore surpassed the generosity of all the martyrs who offered their own lives, because she offered the life of her Son, whom she loved and esteemed infinitely more than herself. Can we find any creature who loved us as she loved us? No creature except Mary, says Saint Bonaventure, was ever so inflamed with love for us, as to give unto us and offer for us her only Son, whom she loved far more than herself.

Many and great are the benefits she has thereby procured and obtained for us. After drawing God from Heaven and earth; after making Him capable of suffering; after sacrificing Him for us, she procures for us the table, the heavenly table, where she gives us to eat and drink nothing less than the Flesh and Blood of God, which is also her flesh and her blood. This Bread is the bread of the Virgin, says Richard of Saint Laurence. *(Lib. 71)*. Therefore she may with truth say: "Come, eat my bread and drink the wine which I have mingled for you." *(Prov. 9:5)*. She has opened unto us the gates of Heaven, and shut those of Hell. She has provided for us the means, helps, Sacraments, and remedies for our weakness and infirmity, with which to work out our eternal salvation. And now that she has become the Arbiter of the Divine Power and Mercy, can you imagine that she does not labor for our advantage and profit, for our well-being in time and in eternity? The power and effects of such immense love are beyond our expression, beyond our comprehension, and I should never end if I should speak of them all. Let us pass, then, to the consideration of the constancy and fidelity of her love for us, and, to avoid too great prolixity, let us reserve this subject for the next chapter.

Twenty-First Day

THE FIDELITY, CONSTANCY, AND
TENDERNESS OF THE LOVE OF MARY

"Love is strong as death." (*Cant.* 8:6). Death is unconquerable. There is no created power that can resist it, prevent it, or even delay it for long: no obstacle can shake its constancy. Such is love, if it be true love, constant in its attachment and fidelity to the object beloved, and strong in surmounting all obstacles that may cross it. The love of creatures, for the most part, wants this condition: a light suspicion, an incautious word, a negligent act, a view of greater interest, pleasure, esteem, or utility, is enough to cool or extinguish it, and sometimes even change it into violent hatred. And if this love is based on the purely natural qualities of beauty, grace, interest, vanity, or ambition; as years increase, as the face becomes wrinkled and the hair turns gray, as interest subsides, and the support of hope grows weak, love becomes lukewarm, then cools, and at last entirely disappears.

Daily experience, facts which have happened, and which happen every day, establish the truth of what I have advanced. The perfidious Herod loved his beautiful wife Mariamne to so strange an excess, that twice he gave orders that she should be put to death when he died, so that no other might possess her; but a single suspicion sufficed to condemn her to public punishment. (*Josephus*). Berenice was foolishly idolized by the Emperor Titus, and yet he drove her an exile from Rome, for fear of displeasing the Romans, and of losing the empire by retaining her. *(Sueton. in Tit.).* Henry VIII loved Anne Boleyn so greatly as to sacrifice for her his conscience, his soul, his religion, and God; yet as soon as he knew she had been unfaithful to him, he had her publicly beheaded, as she richly deserved. The Earl of Essex, the great favorite of Elizabeth, the oracle of her court, and almost king through her favor, was condemned by the queen to an infamous death upon slight suspicion. Behold how inconstant, how changeable is earthly love! Histories are full of similar, and even more remarkable instances; and whole libraries might be filled with the accounts of such cases as have happened, and do daily happen. Well did the poets feign that love was born of the wind and the rainbow, to mark its fickleness and inconstancy!

But it is not so with the love of the Virgin Mary, in whom there is no change, nor shadow of vicissitude. She loved us as soon as she knew us, and she knew us as soon as she was conceived. She has loved us constantly, faithfully, strongly, and tenderly, for almost 18 centuries. She loves us at present with an invincible love; she continues, and will eternally continue, to love us most ardently, if we will but wish it, and not resolve scornfully to tear ourselves from her arms, from her loving bosom, and at the same time from our good. Neither our low and vile condition, nor our misery and poverty, neither disgraces nor sufferings, infamy nor dishonor, natural defects nor failings, neither age nor youth, infirmity nor death itself, can cool in the least the ardor of her love. Whether we are noble or ignoble, rich or poor, fortunate or disgraced, glorious or without fame; though lame, blind, deaf and dumb, foolish and ignorant; whether young or old, strong or weak, sick or well, living or dead, Mary loves us, and will never cease to love us.

Poor child, unfortunate creature, born in the lowest condition, brought up in poverty and miseries, crippled in all your limbs, afflicted with ten thousand infirmities and diseases, abandoned by everyone, scorned and contemned by all; you who seem the refuse and opprobrium of the world; you, yes, you are, if you wish, the object the most loved by the Empress of the World; and your very abjectness, your miseries, disgraces, deformities, which render you so vile, so abject, and so contemned in the eyes of men, make you most dear to Mary, and cause that Most Tender Heart to love you more faithfully, more constantly, and more tenderly; because she sees in you a more express image of her Divine Son, who for us became the opprobrium of men, and the outcast of the people.

But will you believe me, Parthenius, when I tell you that Mary's love is not cooled, is not extinguished even by our ingratitude, infidelity, contempt, nor the most atrocious iniquities? You may well believe it, since you and I have but too often experienced it. Oh! What ingratitude, infidelity, contempt, and injuries she has had to suffer for so many years, so many and many times from me! It has passed all sufferance, and yet has not wearied her patience! She has continued to love me, and still loves me with the same ardor; she has protected and defended me from the just anger of God; she has loaded me with benefits, with spiritual and temporal graces; she pities and excuses me; she consoles and embraces me. And if I desert and offend her a thousand times daily, she lovingly receives me in her arms a thousand times, if I return to her. She once said to Saint Bridget: "However often a man may sin, if he return to me with true and heartfelt penitence, I am ever ready to receive him; and I do not regard the number of his sins, but the intention and will with which he returns." *(Revel. l. ii, c. 23)*. Oh! This is love as strong as death, which the waters of the basest treachery and ingratitude, of the falsest infidelity, cannot extinguish, nor the floods of the most revolting crimes absorb and drown. "Many waters cannot quench charity, neither can the floods drown it." *(Cant. 8)*.

Let us now consider the last of the principal qualities and conditions of true love, which consists in tenderness of expression and of deed, in the most affectionate marks of a truly loving heart. And here, Parthenius, how shall I express the tenderness, the sweetness of the Holy Virgin? It exceeds honey and the honeycomb. Milk and honey are under her tongue, and her lips are as a dropping honeycomb. *(Cant. 4:11)*. I have already *(Chapter 4)* spoken to you of the internal sweetness and consolation which she communicates to loving souls; of the consoling words with which she comforts, rejoices, and rewards the heart of him who loves her. The facts related in a hundred and a thousand places by authors worthy of credit, and which you have perhaps read, are sufficient proof of what I say.

She visits, caresses, and wipes the sweat from the brows of Cistercian monks, wearied with working in the field. *(Spec. exempl. ver. Laborare, ex. 70)*. She visits and consoles in like manner a dying priest, who had wept over her sorrows. *(Cantipr. lib. Ap. apud Sin. cons. 9)*. She appears to a young man who had sighed after her, and carries him with her to enjoy Heaven for all eternity. *(P. Silv. Razzi, part 3, mir. 60)*. She makes a Cistercian monk, called Thomas, who ardently desired to see her, enjoy a paradise upon earth by her most sweet presence. *(Diotall. tom. 2, Tratten. 16).* A poor monk is reduced almost to despair by scruples; she appears to him, and consoles him with these words: "Why, my son, art thou overcome with grief, who hast so often wept with me in mine?" And to console him she takes him with her to Heaven. *(P. Engelgrave, Dom. infra Oct. Nat. § 2).* Two religious of the order of St. Francis lose their way at night in the woods, and she provides them with a magnificent palace and delicious refreshments. *(Nelle cron. apud Lig. Glor. of Mary).* She most gratefully restores to a priest his tongue, which the heretics had cut out because they found him saying Mass in her honor on Saturday. *(Caesar. Dial. lib. 7, c. 24).* The brother of the King of Hungary is obliged by the people to be married; she makes her loving complaint to him while he is saying her office, at the Anthem, "Thou art all fair": "And if I am so fair and beautiful as thou sayest, why dost thou leave me for a far less beautiful spouse?" *(St. Anselm. in ep. apud Auriem, t. 1, e. 8).* She presses to her bosom Saint Bernard, Saint Dominic, Saint Fulbert, Blessed Alain, and many others. *(Diotall. Trattenim, tom. 3, e. 76).*

Oh! These indeed are favors! This is love! Can any love be more disinterested, more powerful, more faithful, more constant, and more affectionate than the Virgin Mary's? With reason does she call herself the Mother of Fair Love; for fairer, sweeter love is not possible in a creature. And yet we make so little account of it, care so little for it, that we do not blush to prefer to it the love of the vilest beings of this earth, who perhaps do not love us at all, and even detest us; or if they seem to love us, it is only for their own interest and advantage, for their own satisfaction or vanity. They cannot procure us a single good; they are oftener the cause and occasion of our miseries, of a thousand misfortunes and calamities, both temporal and eternal. They are most inconstant and faithless, deceitful and beguiling, even at the very time they are giving us the most tender pledge of their love and affection.

Let us love her, Parthenius, who loves us, and loves us incomparably more than all the mothers, sisters, and wives, more than all the angels and the blessed, and all creatures together; who loves us with a love that is disinterested, powerful, constant, and tender. If we love her we shall be most happy in life and most blessed in death, which I pray the Mother of Fair Love may be the lot of us all.

Twenty-Second Day

HOW THE BLESSED VIRGIN RETURNS THE LOVE WE BEAR HER, AND HOW MUCH SHE LOVES THOSE WHO LOVE HER

We have seen, Parthenius, how immense is the love which the Most Holy Virgin has for us; let us now examine how she corresponds to the love which we bear her, and how much more she loves those who love her. If Mary loves us strongly in spite of our ingratitude, and although we do not love her, you may judge how she would love us, and tenderly cherish us, if we truly loved her, if we really desired to please her and to love her, if not as much as she merits, at least to the extent of our strength and ability. She would then expand her heart towards us, and unlock the streams and torrents of her kindnesses. That this is infallibly true, there can be no doubt.

Ingratitude is so horrible a monster, so detestable a vice, that it is abhorred and punished even by the most irrational and savage beasts. Saint Augustine, in the *City of God,* relates a fact which is so strange that it would seem incredible, if it were not written by so great and holy a doctor. An Egyptian lady, he says, fostered a brood of asps in her house, and treated them like pet dogs. One day, when she was gone out, one of the young asps bit an infant lying in the cradle, and killed it. The lady, on returning to her house and finding her child dead, gave vent to her despair, when the mother of the asp which had been guilty of such ingratitude killed it at her feet, a just punishment for its ingratitude to its benefactress.

Yet, Parthenius, the world is full of ingratitude: we read of facts which horrify our nature; such is that related by Segneri, of a soldier who, being hanged but not yet dead, was cut down and restored to life by another soldier who happened to be passing, and who placed him behind him on his horse, in order that he might more easily make his escape. While riding behind his kind liberator, the ungrateful wretch quietly possessed himself of his dagger, and with the very same weapon which had saved his life he took that of his benefactor. Then robbing him of his money, his arms, and his clothes, he left him on the road as food for the dogs and the crows, and rode away on the horse of his murdered benefactor. History is full of similar examples.

This abominable vice, with which men are so infected, is only equalled by the gratitude of Mary, which is even immensely greater than man's ingratitude. Even the least service done her, the least act of respect to her, is rewarded a thousand-fold in this life and in the next. "Thou who art most bountiful, dost return great favors for small services," says Andrew of Crete. So great is her love for us and her desire to benefit us, that the greatest delight we can cause her is to give her an occasion to help us, and she pours her favors richly upon us. She exercised the virtue of gratitude in the highest degree when in this life, and she continues to practice it to the most unlimited extent in Heaven.

I am most certain that no one has ever done the least thing for Mary which has not been abundantly rewarded in this life or in the next. "The Glorious Virgin Mary is most kind and grateful," says Saint Ber-

nardine, "for she will not even suffer a salutation to
pass unanswered. If you say a thousand times, 'Hail
Mary,' she will return your salutation as often." She
thus returned the salutation of Adam of Saint Victor,
who hailed her as Mother of Mercy. She came from
Heaven to thank Father Martin Guttierez, of the
Society of Jesus, for publicly maintaining that her
merits were greater than those of all the blessed
together. Nothing could be more affecting than the
gratitude she showed towards St. Ildephonsus, bishop
of Toledo, for defending the doctrine of her virginity
against the Helvidian heretics, whom he most learn-
edly confuted and drove out of Spain. While Ildephonsus was praying before the tomb of the holy
virgin Leocadia, at the solemn celebration of her
festival, the tomb was miraculously opened, and the
saint appeared to him, and in the presence of the
Viceroy and a great multitude of people, publicly
thanked him, in the name of the Most Holy Virgin, for
his defense of Mary's virginity; she ended with these
words, which are now found in Ildephonsus' office in
the Breviary: "My Lady, who rules in Heaven, hath
gained the victory for thee, Ildephonsus."

The Holy Virgin Mary bent her head to John Duns
Scotus to thank him for his defense of her Immaculate
Conception. In the year 1648 a nobleman of Naples
had a slave named Abel, who was an obstinate
Mahometan. This Abel had quite an affection for an
image of the Holy Virgin which was painted on the
wall in the garden, and took great pleasure in lighting
the lamps before it. She recompensed this attention
by appearing to him with Saint Joseph. "Do you know
me?" she asked. "Yes," he replied, "you are the lady
painted on the wall." "You are right," she said, "and I
am come to tell you that you must be a Christian."

"That I will not," replied Abel. "Yes you will," said Mary, as she placed her hand affectionately on his shoulder; "you will become a Christian, and take the name of Joseph, in honor of my spouse whom you see here with me." She then taught him to make the sign of the cross, and before she left him he besought her to console him whenever he should be afflicted, and she promised to do so, and kept her promise.

But if Mary is so grateful for every little service we do her, what gratitude must she not show him who sincerely and cordially loves her, and gives her the most humble and respectful proofs of his service and love? She loves all in general; but those who, with a special desire to serve her, with a tender affection, and with fidelity, consecrate themselves to her love, and place their whole confidence in her—these indeed are the most precious jewels in her crown, the richest portion of her inheritance, and the most sensitive portion of her heart: her especial, her dearest, her choicest favorites. *Ego diligentes me diligo.* "I love," she says, "them that love me"—and she not only loves them, but she *cherishes* them with the partiality and the tenderness of a mother and a spouse. The word *diligere,* which she here uses, signifies much more than *amare,* since *amare* is a common term for love of all sorts, however low its sphere or ordinary its character; but *diligere* signifies a very strong, special, and most partial love, and distinguishes and selects the one loved, and prefers him to all others. Mary is not satisfied with saying she merely loves those that love her, *Ego amantes me amo,* but, *Ego diligentes me diligo;* thus she declares that she distinguishes and selects them and prefers them to everyone else, in graces, favors, love, and protection. "The Holy Virgin acknowledges," says Saint Bernard *(Serm. super Salve*

Regina), "and dearly loves them that love her, and she is near them that call upon her, especially those whom she sees like her in chastity and humility, and who, after her Divine Son, have placed their whole hope in her." She desires to be loved; she goes before, entices, seeks after someone to give her his heart. She entreats him, "My son, give me thy heart." (*Prov.* 23:26). "She preventeth them that covet her, so that she first showeth herself unto them." (*Wisd.* 6:14). "She seeks for those," says the great Saint Bonaventure *(Stimul. Divin. Amor., p. 3, c. 16),* "who devoutly and reverently approach her; these she cherishes, these she adopts as her children." And, in fact, the demonstrations and expressions of love which Our Blessed Lady has deigned to use with her lovers, are most wonderful. They seem almost incredible. In the preceding chapter we have related a great many, and we will give a few more here in confirmation of her loving gratitude and most partial tenderness towards whomsoever consecrates his heart to her love.

A Spanish youth of the Cistercian Order had dedicated himself entirely to the service and love of Mary, so that he had her ever in his thoughts, in his heart, and on his lips. He became seriously sick, so that his recovery was beyond all hope, and while he was in this state the Most Holy Virgin, his Lady and his Love, appeared to him, and assured him that on the seventh day from that she would return and receive his soul. When the seven days were passed, the prior of the monastery saw during the night a company of most beautiful young men, all clothed in white, come to receive and accompany the soul of the fortunate youth, who, full of joy, amid the melodies of the angels, breathed forth his happy soul into the arms of his Beloved Lady. *(Pelbart. Nierem. L'honer. Bibl.*

Man). A lover of Mary became so enamored of her
beauty and merit, that his life was no more than a continual death, amid sighs and tears. He wept and la-
mented so greatly, that he at last moved the kind
Virgin to compassion; and one day, when he had
prayed and wept more than usual, she appeared to
console him, seated in all her beauty on a throne of
seraphim. The devout lover, being unable to restrain
himself at such tenderness and return of love, was so
overcome by the vehemence of his ardor, that, lost in
a sea of love and contentedness, he breathed forth his
happy soul.

Behold with what promptness and delight Mary
returns the affection of them who love her! Unhappy
that we are! We sometimes lose ourselves for
creatures that value not, care not, for our affection,
who are not pleased with our service, and perhaps
contemn and laugh at our most passionate attachment
to them, and our most heartfelt and tender expressions; and who are not even grateful for our valuable
presents, which they consider simply their due. And
shall we not resolve to love her who, possessing little
less than infinite merit, yet loves us so tenderly, so
earnestly desires our heart, is pleased with our affection, and responds to our love with the most obliging
demonstrations of gratitude, the most constant
fidelity, and who brings about effects which are the
most advantageous to our highest interests? Let us no
longer be so foolish. Let us love Mary, who alone can
make us contented and happy in this world by her
love, and forever blessed in the next by the enjoyment
of her and of God.

Twenty-Third Day

THE COMPASSION AND MERCY OF MARY

One of the most sure signs and effects of a true, strong, and faithful love, is to compassionate and assist the beloved in all his difficulties, labors, dangers, and sicknesses of mind or of body. What is there a mother will not do if her child is in danger? She will spare no labor, not even her safety or her life, to free him. What will not a wife, that truly loves her husband, say and do through pity and compassion for him, if he is in any great affliction or trouble, and most especially if he is in danger of his life?

Baldwin II, emperor of the East, having fallen into the power of the Sultan of Egypt, and being held prisoner by him, Mary his wife travelled over all Europe to solicit from the princes the exorbitant ransom demanded for him by the barbarian. She obtained large sums from the Pope and from the King of France, but these not being enough, she went to her cousin, Alphonsus X, called the Wise, king of Spain. She refused to sit down to the table to take any refreshment with him, saying that she had taken an oath not to sit at table until she had obtained the freedom of her dear lord. Alphonsus was so affected by this proof of her love for her husband, that he made her return the money she had received from the Pope and from the King of France, and paid the whole ransom himself, to the great admiration of all Europe. *(Foresti, Life of Alph. X, A.D. 1267).* Guy, the baron of Rocque de Guy, on the Seine in France, married the daughter of William, a Norman noble of high rank, but of a cruel and barbarous disposition. The latter conceived the desire to become master of the territory of Guy, his son-in-law. For this purpose, with pretended devotion, he went, accompanied by his armed satellites, to the church where his son-in-law was in the habit of attending the divine service. Guy came as usual accompanied by his wife, but had scarce entered the church when he met his father-in-law, who, with his own hand, shut the door behind him to prevent his escape, and he was surrounded and attacked on all sides. The wife, seeing her husband fall under their blows, interposed with prayers and weeping; but finding all in vain, she threw herself upon him to shield him with her own body from their attack, but was forced from him, and he was killed by their repeated blows. The disconsolate lady then threw herself upon his body, and bathed in her own and his blood, she breathed forth her soul on his bosom, as though she had hoped to revive him with her life. *(Foresti, Life of Louis VI of France, A.D. 1110).* Jane, the queen of James I of Scotland, endeavored to defend him with her own body when he was attacked by conspirators, and received two mortal wounds in his defense; yet notwithstanding her exertions, he was pierced with 28 stabs. *(Foresti, A.D. 1437).*

The love which Mary has for us is greater than that of all the mothers and wives in the world. With what emotions, then, of tenderest mercy will she not regard and pity our miseries, and hasten to our assistance? We have already, in another part, touched on this point, when treating of the efficacy of the love of our Most Loving Lady; but it is so interesting and tender a subject, that we cannot apply ourselves too attentively to its consideration. We shall reflect then, Parthenius, in this and the two following chapters, on the compassion with which Mary pities and alleviates the sufferings of all, and particularly of sinners.

Mary is Queen. If the Son, who is born of the Virgin, says Saint Athanasius, is King, it is necessary that the Mother who bore Him should be Queen. *(Serm. de Deip.).* The very name of queen, says Albertus Magnus, indicates mercy and care of her subjects, especially the poor. The magnificence of a king or a queen consists, says Seneca, in assisting the needy. And therefore at his consecration, the head of the king is anointed with oil, which is the symbol of mercy, to show that in his government he should, before all things, cherish thoughts of mercy and compassion in regard to his subjects. Compassion and mercy belong then to Mary by virtue of this title. But Mary is not simply a queen, whose duty it is to be just as well as merciful: she is expressly and solely the Queen of Mercy. The whole Church hails her by the title of Mother and Queen of Mercy.

The kingdom of God, says Gerson *(Gio. Gers. P. 3, Tr. 4: S. Magn.),* consists of justice and mercy. The Lord has divided this kingdom with His Mother. He has reserved to Himself the kingdom of justice, but He has given to Mary the kingdom of mercy, ordering all mercies to pass through the hands of Mary, and leaving her to dispense them as she pleases. And before Gerson, Saint Thomas had taught the same thing in his preface to the Canonical Epistles, where he says that when Mary conceived and brought forth the Divine Word, she obtained the half of the kingdom of God by becoming the Queen of Mercy, while He reserved to Himself the kingdom of justice. Bartoli, in his *History of China,* relates that in the city of Pekin, besides the various tribunals of the empire over which the emperor presides, there is also a tribunal of compassion, under the entire control of the empress-mother. From this tribunal she sends every year 15 commissioners, one into each province, to visit the prisons, with orders to pardon and liberate, in the name of the emperor's mother, all criminals deserving of pardon, even though they may have been convicted on their own confession.

This is precisely what God has done with His Most Holy Mother. Reserving to Himself the tribunal of justice, which is one half of His kingdom, He has given to Mary the other half, the tribunal of mercy, constituting her the Universal Asylum and Refuge of the miserable in this world, and the Judge, not to condemn, but to commiserate and pardon the guilty.

We read in the *Revelations* of Saint Bridget, that she heard Christ pressing His Mother to ask some favor of Him, offering her, as another and more beautiful Esther, even the half of His kingdom. Her heart full of compassion for us, she too prayed for mercy; not however like Esther, for the chosen people alone, but for all that might ever have need of it. This her request was granted her, Christ assuring her that whoever should ask mercy through her, should obtain it. *(S. Brig. in Revel. lib. 7. cap. 10)*. She is the Treasurer and Dispenser of the Mercies of God: they are all placed in her hands, to use the expression of Saint Peter Damian. She is truly the Queen and Mother of Mercy, as she called herself when she appeared to a monk of Cluny, and he asked her who she was; she answered, "I am the Mother of Mercy." *(Diotall. tom. 8, tract. 17)*. Rather she is mercy itself, as says Saint Leo: "Mary is so ready to show mercy, that she merits to be called not only merciful, but even mercy itself."

(Serm. i. de Nativit.). And, therefore, Saint Bonaventure, considering that Mary became the Mother of God for the sake of the unfortunate, and that to her is committed the office of dispensing mercies, and considering the great care which she takes of those who need her assistance, as though her sole delight were in the practice of mercy—St. Bonaventure says that when he reflects on her, this quality so far outshines all others that he seems to see only mercy. *(St. Bonav. Stim. Am.).*

This being now established as a most certain truth, let us see how this Merciful Lady employs this authority which has been given her in the kingdom of God, and what use she makes of her dignity of Mother and Queen of Mercy. Mercy, says the Angelical Doctor *(St. Thom. Sum. IIa IIae, Q. 30, art. 1),* is a certain compassion which arises in the heart at the sight of the sufferings of others, and compels and forces us to relieve them if it is in our power. Hence he only is merciful who, when he sees the sufferings of others, not only feels compassion for them, but also relieves them as far as he can. Such is the ignorance and blindness of the creatures of this earth, that they have but little knowledge of the sufferings of others; so great their hard-heartedness and self-love, that they are but little affected by them; their weakness and incapacity are so great, that for the most part they cannot relieve them even if they should wish it, and therefore they have but a small claim to be called merciful.

But Mary, Queen of Mercy, sees all our wants most clearly in God; even the least of them she knows better than we do ourselves; she has the heart of a most tender mother to feel for us, and her power to assist us is without any limit. For this reason there are not, and never will be, any afflictions on this earth which she does not see and compassionate from Heaven, or which she cannot or will not relieve. The heart of Mary, says Saint Jerome, was even in this life so tender and merciful towards men, that she was more afflicted by the sufferings of others, than anyone else by his own sorrows. *(Ep. ad Eust.).* Of this she gave an example when, at the marriage at Cana, the wine failed; touched with compassion for their shame and confusion, she opportunely provides for their need, and takes upon herself, as says Bernardine of Sienna, the care of assisting them, without even waiting to be asked. Do you believe, asks Saint Peter Damian, that she has changed in this respect, now that she has been raised to the highest position in Heaven and declared Queen of Mercy? The thought is incompatible with the great goodness of Mary; such great mercy as hers cannot forget such great misery as ours. *(St. Pet. Dam., Serm. i de Nat. Virg.).* We should rather say with Saint Bonaventure, that great as was the mercy of Mary towards the needy while she was still an exile in this world, it is far greater now that she reigns in Heaven; her mercy is now manifested more plainly by her innumerable benefits, because she sees more plainly the wants of men.

She commiserates us with the most tender pity in all our labors, our difficulties, and temptations. Many are the sensible proofs which she has given of this tender compassion. Her images have often been seen to shed tears, and have been covered with a copious sweat. Thus Cesarius relates that in a city of Brabant, as the people were hearing Mass before her altar, they all saw her image shed tears so plentifully that several cloths were soaked in them.

The same thing happened in the diocese of Spoleto,

near Trevi, where another image of the Virgin was
seen to weep over a great public calamity, and a temple was erected on the place and dedicated to "Our
Lady of Tears." In Rome, and many other cities of
Europe, there are churches consecrated to her under
the title of "Our Lady of Compassion." She has also
shown the tenderness of her pity for the little inconveniences which her faithful lovers submit to, for love
of her. A young religious of the order of Saint Francis,
who was very devout to the Blessed Virgin, having
been engaged all day in distributing charity to
strangers, was overcome by fatigue while reciting his
Rosary in the evening, and fell asleep. The Blessed
Virgin, compassionating him, appeared to him and
kindly said: "My son, thy fidelity and thy love are
sufficient"; thus she left him restored and greatly
consoled. *(Guid. Vangel. del P. Guistinell, es 18).* She
showed the greatest compassion for the poor Christians in Spain, who were held slaves by the barbarous
Moors. Her kind heart could not bear to see them so
afflicted and oppressed without relieving them. She
appeared one night to Saint Peter Nolasco, Saint Raymond of Pennafort, and James, king of Aragon, and by
means of them instituted in the year 1218, the most
merciful Order for the Redemption of Captives, the
principal duty of which was to collect alms from all
parts of Christendom, to ransom Christian slaves from
the service of the infidels.

But Mary is not content with merely pitying us in
our troubles and temptations; she also powerfully
preserves us from the calamities and punishments
which she foresees, and which we richly merit from
the Divine Justice, and delivers us from those into
which we have already fallen. We should be miserable, indeed, if we had not this Strong Tower to shield

us from the blows of offended Justice: this kind Samaritan, who heals our mortal wounds with the oil of her mercy, and binds them in the folds of her unlimited kindness. How often would the world have been reduced to desolation, and we to eternal ruin, by plague, famine, wars, earthquakes, and fires! Blosius relates that Christ was seen in Rome with three lances in His hand, resolved to destroy the Christian world for the sins of the clergy and people; but the Blessed Virgin interposed, promising Him that the preaching of the holy patriarchs, Dominic and Francis, would convert them to penance. *(De Signis eccl. l. 9, c. x).* Cesarius also relates *(Lib. 12, c. x)* that William, a most holy monk of Clairvaux, saw Christ on a throne commanding an angel to sound a trumpet, which shook the whole world. He was about to command the angel to blow the trumpet a second time, but the Most Merciful Mary, knowing that at the second sound of the trumpet the world would be in ruins, threw herself at the feet of her Divine Son and induced Him to defer its destruction. Astolfi relates that in the year 1117 there was in all Europe, especially in Italy, so fierce an earthquake that many believed the end of the world was come; but it finally ceased, through the intercession of the Most Holy Virgin, as was known by the mouth of a baby in Cremona, who was miraculously enabled to speak.

Saint Antoninus says that in A.D. 1220, in the city of Spoleto, a Dominican novice of noble birth, of great simplicity and purity, and a most devout servant of Mary, one night when he was sleeping saw Christ Our Lord sitting on a throne of great majesty, with His Most Holy Mother, and surrounded by the whole court of Heaven; He held in His hand the world, represented by a globe of immense size, against which

He seemed very angry. He commanded an angel to read the good and the evil which had been done in the world. The angel began with the evil, but angered by such a catalogue of crimes and iniquities, Our Lord cried: "Stop! Stop! No more!" and raising His mighty arm He was about to cast the world angrily from Him and devote it to destruction; at the same moment the world trembled violently, and there was so frightful an earthquake in the city and neighborhood of Spoleto, that churches and houses were thrown to the ground. But the Queen of Mercy would not permit the earth to perish, but hastened to hold the arm of the angry Judge, and to sustain the ruinous and falling world. The novice who witnessed this was so greatly frightened that he repeated the prayer: "We fly to thy patronage . . .," and soon after died of fright. *(S. Anton., part 3, inst. lib. 28, cap. v. § 3)*. In the year 1399, as related by the same Saint Antoninus, Christ appeared to a poor simple peasant, who was rich in virtues and merits, and giving him three cloths commanded him to go and dip them in a neighboring fountain. The peasant went in obedience to His command, but found at the fountain a matron of most majestic appearance, who forbade him to wet those cloths. The same thing happened a second time, although Christ had repeated His command. Finally, Our Lord commanded him to return a third time to the fountain, and to do whatever the matron should tell him. She explained to him the mystery of those three cloths, and made him understand that if he had dipped all three into the fountain, all men then living would have perished in punishment of their sins and excesses, which had justly angered God, but that she, by her prayers and intercession, had obtained that at least two-thirds should find mercy and be saved. She then told him to dip only one of the cloths in the fountain and to make known what he had seen and heard, and to exhort men to penance. His exhortations had such great effect that Saint Antoninus says that the marks of true and public penitence "would appear incredible if we had not seen them with our own eyes." The next year there was so fierce and malignant a pestilence throughout the whole world, that it was the general opinion that a third part of mankind died in that year. That they did not all die was due to the prayers of the Mother of Mercy, who saved two-thirds from the punishment they had all deserved, and obtained for those who died time to prepare themselves for death, so that the punishment might be temporal and not eternal.

We will relate one more fact, and then finish this chapter, to pass to the consideration of the immense mercy of Mary, especially towards poor sinners. At the siege of Perugia, the blessed Columba of Rieti, of the order of Saint Dominic, had recourse to the assistance of the Blessed Virgin, and during her prayer she had this vision; she saw Christ standing on a throne, with an angry look; He had three swords in His hand, and was about to rush upon that poor city, when the Mother of Mercy, seeing the imminent danger it was in, interceded for its pardon. But the Son was too angry to yield to her prayers. She, with the confidence of a mother, ascended the throne, and with easy violence wrested from His hand two of those swords, by which blessed Columba understood that two-thirds of the punishment would be pardoned to the Perugians. And so it happened; for the enemy entering the city were unable to pillage it, or to slaughter the inhabitants as they had intended, and the Perugians deserved. In commemoration of this benefit, they caused the vision to be expressed in several paintings, which were preserved in different churches, and were kept with the greatest veneration, and carried in procession in time of public calamity. *(Diar. Rom. 30, Mag.).*

'Twas thy mercy, O Mary, that we were not destroyed, as would have happened more than once if thou hadst not interposed thy ever-ready assistance as an impenetrable shield to the darts and thunderbolts of Divine Justice!

Twenty-Fourth Day

THE GREAT MERCY OF MARY, PARTICULARLY TOWARDS SINNERS

The kingdom of mercy, Parthenius, would be of no use if there were none who needed mercy; because it would be a kingdom without subjects. "Who are the subjects of mercy," asks Saint Bernard, "if not the miserable?" The kingdom of Mary, Queen of Mercy, is immense, and extends over the whole earth; because the whole earth is full of miseries. But of all miseries, the greatest is sin; of all who are miserable, the most miserable are sinners. Over these, more than all others, does Mary, the Queen of Mercy, exercise her power and command. These are the subjects who most of all oppress her heart, and employ all her cares, all her thoughts, and all her authority, in order to liberate them from their extreme miseries and render them happy and blessed, provided they only desire it. These are the most precious gems of her royal crown. "Come from Libanus, my spouse; come from Libanus, come," says the Holy Ghost, her Spouse. "Thou shalt be crowned . . . from the dens of the lions, from the mountains of the leopards." (*Cant.* 4:8). Why should her crown be so monstrous, so horrible, composed of lions, of leopards, tigers, and wild beasts? These monsters, these wild beasts, are the bright gems in the crown of the Queen of Mercy; for these monsters and these wild beasts are sinners, whom Mary has converted and saved. "Thou shalt be crowned from the dens of these lions," says Rupert the Abbot; "for their salvation shall be thy crown." Saint Gertrude once saw this Most Merciful Lady with her mantle spread out, and under it lions, bears, tigers, and many other wild beasts, who were gathered together and protected by Mary, with the greatest kindness; and the saint understood that those wild beasts were sinners, not yet lost, on whom Mary exercises her most tender compassion.

In the first place, she feels for their sufferings; and like a mother who loves her son, though the sinners are covered with wounds and leprosy, she is grieved and afflicted at their unhappy state, and the great danger they are in of losing their life and their salvation. She sees the fair image of herself, and of God their Father, deformed in them; she beholds them pierced by their most cruel enemy, by thousands and thousands of mortal wounds; she sees them about to precipitate themselves into an abyss of eternal torment and pain; she considers that they were the work of the hand of the Creator, that they were redeemed at the price of the sufferings and Blood and precious life of her Divine Son and herself, and she is afflicted at the sight of their most miserable state, and the imminent danger they are in of eternal ruin. She has often given the most plain and certain marks of her tender compassion to sinners themselves, as when an image of her, with seven swords in the breast, in sign of her seven principal sorrows, appeared one morning pierced by eight swords to a pious youth who was accustomed to visit it every day, and he heard at the same time a voice which said that the sin he had committed the night before, had added the eighth sword to the heart of Mary. *(P. Roviglia)*. Thus, also, a lady, who was most obstinate in refusing to confess a certain sin, though she should be damned for it, saw an image of Mary weeping, and moved by those mysterious tears asked why she wept, and heard a voice which answered: "I weep out of compassion for thy soul, which is destroying itself by its obstinacy." The lady, moved to contrition, begged pardon of the Virgin, and went immediately to confession to confess her sin to God.

Mary mitigates the anger of God and suspends His punishments. Wretched sinners! God stands over you, ready in His anger to condemn you to eternal damnation: on one side of you is death, ready to cut the thread of your life at the first signal of the Almighty; on the other hand is the devil, awaiting that blow to cast you into endless torments; under you, Hell opens its jaws to swallow you; within you, is sin crying to Heaven for vengeance upon you; and around you are earthquakes, plagues, famines, pestilences, wars, wild beasts, and all creatures ready to execute the sentence of divine justice. "Who hath showed you to flee from the wrath to come?" (*Matt.* 3:7). Who will save you? Oh! Run, fly; but whither? To the bosom of Mary; she is the City of Refuge, your only hope. There were many cities of refuge in Judaea, but not all crimes nor all persons were safe there. We have but one city, but in it all find safety, no matter what crimes they may have committed. Our Lord complained to Ezechiel that there was no one who opposed His anger: "I sought among them for a man that might set up a hedge, and stand in the gap before Me in favor of the land, that I might not destroy it; and I found none." (*Ezech.* 22:30). But there is one found at last who will hold Him and pacify Him, and this one is Mary. She is, says Pelbart, like a mother when she sees her children in danger of punishment from their father. They fly to their mother, who folds them in her arms, and shields them from the anger and punishment of their father. In the same manner Mary receives to her bosom sinners who recur to her; she hides them under her mantle until she has pacified the anger of God, and reconciled them to Him. She declared also to Saint Bridget, that she is the Mother of all sinners, and that she is always ready to undertake their defense; and is like a kind mother, who when she sees her child running to her to escape from his enemies who are pursuing him with drawn swords, places herself between him and the danger which threatened him.

This kind protection of Mary was experienced in a most signal manner by a young man, who while travelling with two companions was overtaken by a severe storm. He heard a voice in the air say: "Strike! Strike!" And immediately one of his companions fell, struck by lightning. The same also happened to the second. The young man then had recourse to the protection of the Holy Virgin, and when the voice again commanded: "Strike! Strike!" another voice replied: "I cannot; I cannot."

She also weakens the strength of sinners' passions; removes from them the dangers and occasions of sin; lessens the violence of their temptations; restrains the fury of their infernal enemies, so that the poor sinners either are less tempted, or sin less than they otherwise would. "There is no sinner living," she said to Saint Bridget, "that is so accursed and forsaken as to be deprived of my mercy; for, through my intercession, everyone receives the grace to be less tempted than he would be without it." *(Lib. i. c. 6)*. And she has sometimes even made use of a miraculous power to preserve them from new lapses, as happened to one who, on approaching the door of a house where he was in manifest danger of falling again, felt himself held back by an invisible power, and prevented from entering.

Mary frees sinners from the violence of their passions, breaks the chains of their vices and evil habits, delivers them from the slavery of the devil, though they may have voluntarily entered it; and even brings them back from the path to Hell. Innumerable facts which prove my assertion, are related by every writer on this subject; but of these I will select only a few for your edification.

Father Segneri *(Crist. istr. p. 111, rag. 34)* relates that a young nobleman of Rome, who was loaded with sins of impurity, and bound by the chains of inveterate bad habits, went to confession to Father Nicholas Zucchi. The holy priest saw clearly that there was but little hope for his cure unless the Most Holy Virgin could be induced to undertake his case. The priest therefore imposed for his penance that, until his next confession, he should repeat one "Hail Mary" every morning and evening, and offer to the Mother of Purity his eyes, his hands, and his whole body, beseeching her to guard them as her own. The young man faithfully performed the penance with but little profit at first; still he continued in it by the advice of the good Father, and while in this state he left Rome, and travelled over the world for many years. Being at last returned, he threw himself at the feet of the good Father Zucchi, thanking him without measure for the good medicine he had given him, and he was found changed into quite another man, being now chaste, continent, and most devout to the Holy Virgin. Nor was this all; for the story, being related from the pulpit, took so strong a hold on a young officer, who was also addicted to this beastly vice, that he resolved to practice the same devotion; and the effect from it was the same, for he soon broke the chains which bound him to sin, and became a pious and edifying servant of Mary.

Eutychian, patriarch of Constantinople, relates a most wonderful instance of the great power of Mary. There was in the city of Cilicia an archdeacon of the church of Adanas, named Theophilus, of so irreproachable a life that the people wished him to be their bishop; but his humility made him refuse the dignity. Being afterwards calumniated and deposed, he became so indignant that he signed a contract delivering his soul to the evil one. Being afterwards sorry for what he had done, he threw himself on the protection of the Blessed Virgin, who appeared to him, consoled him, obtained his pardon, and restored to him the contract which he had made, and which she had forced the devil to return to her, thus delivering Theophilus from the power and slavery of his fiercest enemy, to which he had voluntarily subjected himself.

Saint Peter Damian, reflecting on this example, exclaims, "O Mary, who couldst snatch Theophilus from the very jaws of perdition, what is there that thou canst not do?" *(Serm. i, de Nat. Virg.)*. She delivered Father Bartholomew Cesena from a great lake of fire, into which he had fallen in punishment for his wicked life, as is related in the Annals of the Capuchins. *(An. 1592)*. And although this was only in a vision and a wandering of his senses, I still firmly believe that Mary would bring back souls from Hell, if from that prison of torment they could only turn to her for mercy and assistance; and I am still more strengthened in this belief by what Saint Gertrude once heard Christ say to His Mother, that He would be ready to show mercy even to Lucifer, and obtain his pardon, if he would only ask her assistance with humility.

But what she cannot do for the devil and the reprobate, because they will not humble themselves, and because all repentance is over for them, she does daily for sinners in this world, to prevent their falling into those endless sufferings. She enlightens and excites their understanding, softens and moves their will, and almost forces them to repent and be converted. Thus she appeared to Henry del Castro, of the order of Saint Dominic, as he was going to say Mass, and told him first to confess a certain sin which he had passed over as of small importance.

The annual letters of the Society of Jesus for the year 1560 relate that a man, who had fallen into a great sin, which he was so ashamed of that he was determined to die and be lost rather than confess it, was struck on the shoulder by an invisible hand while asleep, and heard a distinct voice commanding him to go to confession. He had recourse to the Blessed Virgin, and his heart was suddenly changed, his vain apprehension vanished, and he obtained a complete victory over himself. A wicked woman named Helen merely recited her Rosary, without any devotion, and in return the Holy Virgin filled her soul with such sweet consolation, and horror for her past life, that she went to confession, and accused herself of her sins with such great sorrow and contrition, that she came near fainting in the confessional: and she was afterwards warned by Mary of the approach of death; and when it came, it found her prepared. The Holy Virgin granted the same grace to Catherine the Fair, a notorious sinner in Rome, for saying a few prayers in her honor; to Saint Mary of Egypt, and thousands of others, who like them were lost in their sins, and who despaired of pardon. With reason, then, did Mary call herself the "Magnet of Hearts" to Saint Bridget *(Rev., lib. 3, c. 32);* for as the magnet draws iron, so does she attract all hearts, and draw them violently to her, that she may reconcile them to God. She is the mystical Ruth who hath found grace in the eyes of God, to glean after the reapers the ears of grain which are rebellious souls, hardened and despairing sinners, who are not converted by the missionaries and preachers. "Mary," says Saint Bonaventure, "does not abandon the greatest sinner; if he will but call on her, she will raise him from the depths of his despair." *(Pan. B. V.).* Denis the Carthusian calls her "the Especial Refuge of the Lost, the Hope of the Miserable, and the Advocate of all Sinners who fly to her." No one is excluded and abandoned by her mercy, just as there is no one who does not feel the heat of the sun, to which she is compared in the Old Testament: she is "chosen as the sun," and there is no one that can hide himself from her heat. (See *Ps.* 18).

One of the Fathers of the Congregation of the Most Holy Redeemer was one day in the confessional, when he saw a young man who seemed to hesitate, to wish and yet to be unwilling to confess. The good priest called him to him, and asked him if he wished to confess. "Yes," answered the youth, "but I do not know as God will pardon me." Being encouraged by the confessor, he began: "You must know, Father, that besides innumerable sins of impurity, murder, and other crimes, I despaired of my salvation, and began to commit sin for the sake of offending God, and for no other cause than the hatred which I bore Him." He said that he had received Communion that same morning, for the purpose of trampling the consecrat-

ed Host under his feet, and that he was only prevented from doing so by the number of people who
were looking at him; and he gave the priest the
Sacred Particle, wrapped in a piece of paper. He said
that he was passing the church, and felt an impulse to
enter: seeing others confessing, he came forward; but
being still undecided, he wanted to go away, but was
detained he knew not how; when the priest called
him he approached, and was now at his feet, but yet
he hardly believed it. Being asked if he ever practiced any devotion to the Blessed Virgin, he said,
"None, except that I have always worn her scapular."
"That has saved you," said the priest. The young man
was so moved by the thought of such great mercy,
that, with many tears, he made a general confession of
his whole life; and at the end of it was so overcome by
sorrow and contrition, that he fainted at the feet of his
confessor. After he was restored to consciousness he
received absolution, and gave the priest permission to
publish this miracle of the mercy of God and of His
Holy Mother. *(Lig. Glor. of Mary).*

Saint Vincent of Ferrera visited a sinner who was
dying in despair. "Why," he asked him, "do you wish
to damn yourself, when Jesus Christ wishes to save
you?" The sick man replied that it was to spite Jesus
Christ that he wished to be damned. "But to spite
yourself you must be saved," said Saint Vincent, who
commenced reciting the Rosary with the rest of the
household. The sick man soon afterward asked to be
allowed to make his confession, which he did with
many tears of contrition; and after he had received
absolution, he died.

O Mary, the Hope of the Despairing, the Protector
of the Condemned, who will not hope in thee, since
thou savest those who have lost all hope?

Twenty-Fifth Day

Not content with converting sinners, Mary also obtains from God their pardon, which He might justly refuse to them. Through her intercession we obtain the pardon of our sins. Saint Bernard *(Sup. Salve Regina)*, therefore, exhorts sinners "to have recourse to her," assuring them that she will show to her Son the breast which gave Him milk, and He cannot deny her their pardon. In the diary of the Blessed Virgin for the 14th of March, it is related that a sinner, praying to her to obtain his pardon, and shedding many tears, was answered when Mary collected the tears in a white linen and presented them to Christ, saying, "Wilt Thou suffer these tears to flow in vain?" and she thus obtained the pardon she asked.

We also read in the same place that Saint Peter of Crescia, after the death of his father, conceived a most extraordinary sorrow for the sins of his youth, and before confessing he recurred to the Virgin and besought her to obtain his pardon. His prayer was heard, for he had scarce knelt in the confessional when he heard a voice from Heaven say, "Thy sins are forgiven thee." Her merits with her Divine Son are so great, that she can easily supply our want of merit, and what is denied us will be granted to her. Many are the instances we read of where Christ, inexorable to sinners, has yielded to the prayers of Mary and granted their pardon.

The Camaldolese Father Silvano Razzi relates that a monk of the order of Cistercians fell into a sin which gave great scandal. Being very much confused and afflicted for the excess of which he had been guilty, he turned to the Mother of Mercy and besought her to obtain for him the pardon of his sin. One day, while praying, he saw the Glorious Virgin with a Most Beautiful Child in her arms; she was begging Him to take the monk into favor again, but the Child turned away from the monk as though unwilling to be reconciled; but the Tender Mother transferred Him from one arm to the other, thus kindly turning His face again upon the unhappy monk, renewing her prayers and entreaties, till at last she conquered, and the Child, turning His countenance towards the Cistercian, accepted his tears and contrition. Carthagena relates a similar instance of what happened to a soldier sunk in every sort of vice. *(De Mirand. Deip.).* "O Mary," exclaims Saint Bonaventure, "thy maternal heart embraces sinners despised by the whole world, and does not abandon them till they are reconciled to their Judge." *(In Spec. Am., c. 5).* This is one of the great privileges which Jesus Christ has granted to His Mother, that she may obtain the pardon of all sinners who fly to her assistance and invoke her patronage.

After sin has been pardoned, and the eternal punishment due to it remitted, there still remains the temporal punishment which the offended justice of God demands, and which must be expiated either by voluntary penance in this life, or by the purifying torments of Purgatory in the life to come. Even this temporal punishment is diminished by this Loving Queen of Mercy, who shortens it and makes it less intense, or entirely delivers the repentant sinner from it. She is so kind and loving that she cannot bear to see us suffering or in trouble; and, therefore, if she sees the sinner afflicted for his sin, she is immediately moved to compassion and hastens to his relief. I am not now speaking of the torments which the converted sinner must pass through in Purgatory; these I shall speak of in another place. I here refer only to those temporal sufferings which the sinner undergoes in this life for the expiation of his sins. Even from these does Mary wish to free her children; and it seems as though one of the special charges committed to her by God was to satisfy the Divine Justice in our name. When she was in this world she offered herself to God a willing victim for the expiation of the sins of the whole world; and God alone knows to what afflictions, mortifications, labors, and penances she subjected herself, in order to satisfy the Divine Justice for sins not her own. All that she suffered in her own person, or that of her Son, she offered to God in expiation of the sins of the whole world.

Now that she is in Heaven, she cannot suffer for men, but she still importunes God with her prayers and intercession, offering Him the Blood of her Divine Son and her own merits to supply the satisfaction which sinners owe to His offended justice, and free them from the sufferings which they merit. She has delivered many from their punishments, and even from death, to which they had been condemned by human justice. Even those who despised and insulted her have enjoyed the fruits of her mercy. And when it is necessary that sinners should bear the punishment of their sins in this life for their greater good and profit, she does not fail to assist, comfort, and console them, and to obtain for them the help and strength which are necessary to enable them to bear it in such manner that their temporal pains may become for them fruitful merits of eternal recompense.

It is to no purpose that the pilot has bravely and carefully guided the ship through a safe course, that he has kept it uninjured in storms, that he has avoided rocks and shoals, and dangerous contact with others, if he does not safely bring it to the intended port. So also the Queen of Mercy, full of tenderness and compassion for sinners, is not satisfied with defending them from the anger and punishment of God, removing from them the occasions of sin, repressing the violence of their temptations, restraining the fury of their most cruel enemies, breaking their chains, converting them, obtaining for them the pardon of God, and exempting them from the punishment they merit, if she does not also conduct them safe and sound into the port of eternal happiness.

"She is called the Star of the Sea," says Saint Thomas; "because as sailors are guided to their port by the polar star, which is the star of the sea, so also Christians are guided in their voyage to eternal glory by Mary." *(Opusc. 9)*. It would be hard indeed for poor sinners if they were not guided by Mary to their salvation. "By her means they are converted to God, and by her intercession they are saved," says St. Germain. *(De Dor. Deip.)*. "Through thee," says Saint Bernard, "Heaven is opened, Hell emptied, the heavenly Jerusalem restored, and life granted to those who expected only eternal death." *(Serm. 4. de Assumpt.)*. [St. Bernard means that Hell is deprived of souls who would have gone there, had Mary not assisted them.] To this purpose she exerts all her power and authority, and her most efficacious intercession; and she has only to wish it and the sinner will be saved, even though it should require a miracle to effect it.

A poor woman named Mary was so great a sinner in

her youth, and continued so in her old age, that she was driven out of the city where she had lived, and forced to reside in a miserable cave, where she died, abandoned and deserted by everybody, and without the Sacraments. She was not, however, abandoned by Mary, to whom she turned in her last moments; she obtained from her a true contrition for her sins, and was saved, as she revealed to Sister Catherine of Saint Augustine. *(Liguori, Glor. of Mary).* A nobleman who for 60 years had been the slave of the devil, and led a most desperate life, still preserved some little devotion to Mary, and the Lord had mercy on him and converted him by means of a confessor, who was sent to him three times, and he was saved, as was revealed to Saint Bridget. *(P. Eus. Nieremb. Tr. Mar., lib. 4, c. 9).* Alexandra, a noble lady of Aragon, in the midst of her sins retained a devotion to Mary, and remained for a long time at the point of death, but the Holy Virgin would not suffer her to die till she had confessed and received the Bread of Angels by the hand of Saint Dominic.

Only Hope of Sinners, Most Secure Haven of the Shipwrecked, Protectress of the Damned, thou dost save those who have despaired; who, then, will not hope in thee? Who will not love thee? Who hath heard of such wonderful things as Mary, the Queen of Mercy, does in favor of her subjects? Happy are we who live under so blessed a government, and are subjects of so tender a Queen. We are sinners, it is true, but for this very reason we have an especial claim on her mercy and protection. She would not be Queen of Mercy if there were none in her kingdom on whom she could exercise her mercy. It is only necessary that we confide in her, and not abuse her mercy, that we do not wish to continue in our sins, and that we do not wish—confident and presumptuous of her protection—to continue to pierce her heart by our iniquities. For then we should merit that bitter reproof which she made to a sinner who implored her aid: "You sinners call me Mother of Mercy, but by your sins you make me the Mother of Misery." *(Gerem. Erolt. in Prompt.).* But if, penitent for our past transgressions and wishing to amend, we pray to her with confidence, we shall find that "she is meek and sweet not to the just only, but to all, even the greatest sinners, when she sees them fly to her assistance that she may reconcile them to their Judge." *(Blos. in Cant. Vit. Sp., c. 28.).* She helps all those who endeavor to rise to God, and refuses her consolation to none.

Let us help ourselves, Parthenius; let us strive to rise from the bonds of slavery which our sins have brought upon us; let us cry to her, that we may be delivered from our passions and evil habits; let us fly to this Sweet Mother of Pity, this Queen of Mercy, praising her, honoring her, loving her, and invoking her. Let us hold her fast, and not let her go till she blesses us; saying to her with St. Bonaventure, "What shall we fear? Of what shall we be afraid? He that has thee has all that he wants. All who are in need of mercy are subject to thy kingdom. Let me not be deprived of confidence in thee." And she will extend over us her powerful arm, she will break the chains which bind us to sin, she will make us enjoy all the fruits of her mercy, and in the end bring us safely to eternal salvation.

Twenty-Sixth Day

THE LOVE OF THE MOST HOLY VIRGIN IS A
CERTAIN SIGN AND SECURE PLEDGE OF OUR
ETERNAL SALVATION

What a frightful situation, Parthenius, was that in which were placed the two sons of Mahomet II, Sultan of Turkey, when by his order they were compelled to fight each other for the possession of life and the government of that great empire, death and the gibbet being the lot of the one who was conquered! That barbarous monarch had reserved for himself a large tract of country, and forbidden anyone, under pain of death, to hunt within its limits. His two sons, not regarding themselves as included in the decree, did not hesitate to transgress it. Their father heard of it, cast them in prison, and condemned them to death. No one dared to say a word in their favor, except the Mufti, who is the head of their religion. He represented to the Sultan that these two were his only heirs, and in the name of the empire besought him not to deprive them of a successor to the throne. "Well," replied Mahomet, "one successor is enough; let one live and the other be put to death, as an example to all of the obedience which is due to my commands." He accordingly ordered three tables to be prepared in a large hall; the first table was covered with purple, with a turban, a sword, and the ensigns of government; on the second, which was covered with black, were a block and an axe; finally, on the third, which stood in the center, were two swords. To this were the princes led, and while the Sultan, their father, sat majestically on his throne and regarded them with barbarous delight, they fought for life with an empire, or death with dishonor.

But much more terrible, Parthenius, is the situation in which you, and I, and all of us are placed, if we but reflect on the issue of the warfare which we must wage during this life. If we are victorious, eternal life and an everlasting kingdom await us; but if we yield, eternal death and never-ending torment. But, Parthenius, we need not fear the result of this contest, if Mary is on our side, if she fights for us and with us. Our salvation is then secure. Her love is a sign of our predestination.

Mary loves us, and she loves us, as we have shown, with an insuperable and invincible love; more than all the mothers, sisters, and spouses in the world, if they should all unite with one heart to love us. She loves us with a most effectual love, desiring, willing, and procuring our greatest temporal and spiritual good; and what is still more, she loves us although we are ungrateful, faithless, and sinful. How much would she love us, then, if we corresponded to her love, loved her in return, were faithful to her, and gave her our whole confidence, our whole heart! We have seen that she is most grateful, and knows no bounds in her love to those that love her; and loving us in this manner, and so effectually, will she not wish to see us contented and happy? Will she not wish to secure our eternal beatitude? Will she not advocate our cause before the tribunal of Divine Mercy? Will she not incessantly request of God our eternal salvation? Who can doubt it? If she has not permitted those who could no longer live to pass from this life, even requiring a dispensation of the laws of nature to recall those who were almost dead, that they might not perish eternally, merely because they had preserved some shadow of devotion and had placed some confidence in her protection—if she has done even this, will she permit the truly devout, her faithful lovers, to perish? Oh, I should think a doubt so impious, so injurious to her, would be little less than blasphemy!

No, no, Parthenius! She wishes absolutely our salvation; she wishes us to praise and bless her, to thank and love her eternally in Heaven, and therefore she desires and continually prays to her Son for our salvation. And if she wishes it and requests it, will her Son deny it? Will that Son, who has granted her a hundred and a thousand times the salvation of the most obstinate, the most desperate, the most hopeless sinners—will that Son deny her the salvation of her faithful servants, of her tender lovers—that Son who has given her the half of His kingdom, making her Queen and Mother of Mercy, precisely because He wishes all to be saved—that Son who, wishing to redeem the human race, deposited its whole price in her hands *(St. Bernard. De Aquaeduc)*—that Son, who has committed to her the dispensation of His Blood *(S. Anselm)*, that she might dispense it to her children? *(S. Benardin. Sien.)*. Sooner shall the heavens fall and the earth be burnt to ashes.

"It is impossible that the Mother of God should not obtain what she asks of her Son." *(S. Antonin., part 4, tit. 15. c. 17, § 4)*. "What she seeks, she finds, and her prayer is always heard," says Saint Bernard.

And it is certain that if, on an impossible supposition, Mary should demand the salvation of a sinner, and on the other side, all the angels, all the saints, and all the just should demand his condemnation, the sinner would be saved—because Mary alone would be heard. Because, says Saint John Damascen, there is as it were an infinite distance between the Mother of God and His servants; because God loves the Virgin alone more than all the elect; and finally, because the prayers of the saints, as says Saint Antoninus, rest solely on His mercy; but the prayer of Mary rests on her own merits, she having merited *de congruo* for the predestined all the helps of grace *(Recapito, De Sign. Praedestin., c. 12, n. 279)*, and on the right which, as Mother, she has over Christ, who as her Son, by the law of nature and evangelical justice, can deny her nothing. Therefore, he adds, the prayer of the Virgin has almost the force of a command. *(S. Antonin., part 4, tit. 11, c. 17, § 4).* The question is treated by Suarez *(Tom. ii. part 3, disp. 23, sect. 2)*, and solved as I have here explained it; and the Doctors all agree in this, that neither the power nor the will to save us can be wanting to Mary: we shall then be saved.

In confirmation of this necessary conclusion, and for your greater consolation, let us see what the saints and doctors say on this point; and because there are many who treat this subject, I will, without any order of preference, give you them one by one in their very words. And first of all, I meet with the celebrated sentence of Saint Anselm *(De Excell. Virg., c. 11)*, given by Saint Bonaventure *(Specul. Virg., e. 3)*, which for its greater credit, was submitted to the examination of the theologians, and, as Mendoza attests *(Virid., lib. 2, prob. 9)*, was found true in all scholastic rigor. Saint Anselm then says: "O Most Blessed Virgin, as it is impossible for anyone to be saved abandoned by thee, so it is impossible for him to perish who turns to thee, and is regarded by thee."

This is, in truth, Parthenius, a great sentence, and one that should greatly console the lovers of Mary, and take from them all fear and apprehension for their eternal salvation. And Saint Anselm confirms this as his opinion in many places. "It is sufficient that thou desirest our salvation, O Mary, and we cannot but be saved." "He shall not hear the eternal curse, for whom Mary shall pray even once."

After Saint Anselm comes Saint Antoninus, who says the same thing in almost the same words. "As it is impossible that they should be saved from whom Mary turns away the eyes of her mercy, so also it is necessary that they upon whom she turns her eyes, advocating their cause, should be saved and be glorified." *(St. Antonin., part 4, tit. 5).* And here take notice of the word *necessary,* by which he means that those who are devout to Mary must necessarily be saved.

In the third place, comes Saint Bonaventure, who in a great many places agrees with Saint Anselm, saying: "He that perseveres in thy service shall not be lost." "They that love thee, O Lady, shall enjoy much peace; their soul shall not see death forever." *(In Ps. 118).* "To know thee, O Virgin Mother of God, is the way of immortality, and to recount thy virtues is the way of salvation." *(In Ps. 83).* "Give ear, O ye nations, that desire the kingdom of God; honor the Virgin Mary, and you shall find eternal life." *(S. Bonav. in Psalt.).* "They that gain the favor of Mary shall be acknowledged by the citizens of

Heaven; and they that bear the mark of her servants shall be registered in the book of life." *(St. Bonav. in Specul.).* "The gate of Heaven shall be opened to him who has hoped in her." Saint Bernard called the love of Mary, and devotion to her, a certain sign of obtaining eternal salvation. And the blessed Alain says, "This devotion is a sure sign of predestination for the possessor." *(Part 2, Rosar., c. 11).*

Twenty-Seventh Day

The servants of Mary are as sure of paradise as though they were already there, is the bold saying of the Abbate Guerico. *(Liguori, Glor. of Mary)*. "Who are they that are saved and reign in Heaven?" asks Saint Denis the Carthusian; and he replies, "Those surely for whom the Queen of Mercy intercedes." *(Ibid)*. It is not possible, says Blosius *(In Cant. Vit. Spir., c. 18)*, that any devout and humble worshipper of Mary should perish. No one is saved, says Saint Germain *(Serm. de Zona Dom.)*, except through thee, Most Holy Virgin. Saint Ignatius the Martyr used to say that no one will ever perish who devoutly and diligently honors and loves the Virgin Mother of God. *(Lig. Glor. of Mary)*. "He that loves me," says Richard of Saint Laurence, in the person of Mary, "will be loved by the Father and by my Son," which is the same as to be predestined to a beatitude of glory. Our salvation is in her hands, says Jordan. *(In Pr. Contempl. de B. V.)*. But I should never end, if I should try to collect all the sayings of all the saints and doctors on this point; and they are all to the same effect. Suffice it to say, that the devil himself has been forced to acknowledge this truth. For Saint Dominic once exorcised an Albigensian heretic, possessed by devils, in the city of Carcassona in France, and forced them to tell the truth: "Hear, O Christians," cried the devils; "all that our enemy has said of Mary is true, and we

are forced to confess that no one is damned who perseveres in the devotion to Mary." *(P. Pacciuch. Sal.
Aug. Ex. 4, N. 10).*

In short, all the Doctors and Fathers of the Church
unite in extolling the power of her mercy. One calls
her the "Path of Salvation, and the Way that leads to
paradise." *(St. Athanas. Serm. i. de an. Virg.).* Another
calls her the "Ladder to Heaven." *(St. Peter Damian).*
Saint Ephraim calls her the "Opening of the Heavenly
Jerusalem." Saint Bernard and Saint John Geometra
salute her as the "Chariot which carries men to God."
Saint Proculus says she is "a Safe Bridge across the
stormy ocean of this life." And the Holy Church invokes her as the "Star of the Sea," "Gate of Heaven,"
"Our Salvation and Our Life," and applies to her
those passages of Holy Writ which speak of her as a
secure pledge of salvation. "They that work by me,
shall not sin; they that explain me, shall have life
everlasting." *(Ecclus.* 24:30, 31). "He that shall find
me, shall find life, and shall have salvation from the
Lord." *(Prov.* 8:35). "She is a tree of life to them that
lay hold on her; and he that shall retain her is
blessed." *(Prov.* 3:18). Let us lay hold on her then, and
retain her, and not let her go till she bless us.

Although we may have been, and may yet be, sinners, she is still the pledge of our salvation; and we
must not on that account cease to serve her, to honor
her, to love her, and to place our confidence in her;
but rather, on the contrary, we must devote ourselves
all the more earnestly to her service and love. If we
but forsake our sins, or at least have an ardent desire
to do so, and call on her for aid, she will reach us her
hand, and enable us to rise from our iniquities. For this
purpose let us direct to her all our vows, our desires,
and our labors, and she will assuredly obtain for us

grace and perseverance, and in the end everlasting salvation and the joys of eternity.

The examples which I have related, and the opinions of the holy Fathers, of the saints, and Doctors of the Church, which I have quoted, must certainly have so convinced you of the truth of this that there can no longer be any doubt in your mind. It is the unanimous doctrine of the whole Church, and it would not only be a sin, but rashness and impudent boldness on your part to doubt it. Faith teaches it, and reason confirms it; shall we then doubt it? No, Parthenius, let us not doubt it; but let us thank God that He has given us a Mother so willing and able to assist us; and let us pray Him to infuse into our hearts the most tender confidence, the most ardent love, and the most faithful devotion towards her, since this confidence, this love, and this devotion are a special grace which He grants only to those whom He has predestined to eternal salvation. Yes, let us serve, honor, venerate, and love her, and we may lay aside all fear of losing our salvation.

Francis Ottajano, a student of the famous university of Alcala, was most devout to the Blessed Virgin, but was so troubled with doubts of his predestination that he was continually tormented with the most horrible fears of his damnation. He was on the very brink of despair. One day when he had been more than usually troubled by these thoughts, the Blessed Virgin appeared to him, accompanied by a multitude of angels and saints, especially those to whom he was most devout, and said to him: "My son, why dost thou fear? Why dost thou not confide in me? Dost thou not know that I am the Mother of Compassion and Mercy? Look at this book; it is the book of life, in which are written the names of all those that are to be saved. Here is your name placed among those of the predestined, together with the names of all those who will be saved by your preaching." The young man raising his eyes, saw, with infinite delight, his own name written in letters of gold; but however much he tried to read the names of the others, it was impossible for him to do so.

The Amiable Lady then, smiling, shut the book, and giving him her benediction, disappeared; and with her departed all the troubles and melancholy of the young man, who remained so confident of his salvation that he was afterwards accustomed to say, that if he had a promise of his salvation written and signed by the hand of God, he would destroy it, and throw it into the fire, wishing rather to expect it from Divine Goodness and the protection of the Most Holy Virgin, secure of obtaining it. He afterward became a religious of the Society of Jesus, and being sent to the Philippine Islands, converted innumerable souls; and afterwards returning to Rome, died in that city in the odor of sanctity.

O Hope of the Desperate! On whom shall we base the hope of our salvation if not on thee? Let others found it on the testimony of a good conscience, and their innocence, or on a sincere conversion and a penitence proportioned to their sins: I do not wish to rely on either of these. I know that I have sinned many and many times, and I know that I have not appeased the anger of God with even the smallest part of the satisfaction due to His justice; I know how great is my weakness, that I fall at every stumbling block; I know the enemies who persecute me, and the dangers which surround me on all sides—but what then? If I enjoy the shadow of thy amiable protection, I am safe.

On thee I rely; on thee I confide; a single word spoken by thee in my favor will obtain my salvation.

My only fear is, that my ingratitude may cause me to lose thy grace; but I know that thou art most merciful, and that even the ingratitude and infidelity of thy servants is not enough to extinguish the fire of charity in thy heart; and I, although I were a reprobate sinner, wish to continue to serve thee, to praise thee, and to love thee, and not to be separated from thee, either living or dead. "Even though thou shouldst kill me, I will hope in thee" (Cf. *Job* 13:15); though I should be condemned to Hell, I would not cease to call upon thee, and invoke thy assistance (if this were not impossible), most certain that thou wouldst deliver me from that eternal abyss, since I know thou wouldst show mercy even to the devil, if he should ask it. In thee, O Mary, have I hoped; let me not be confounded forever.

Twenty-Eighth Day

THAT THE LOVE OF THE BLESSED VIRGIN INSURES A HAPPY DEATH

What a terrible instant! What a frightful moment! An instant on which depends either eternity of torment or eternity of infinite delight and beatitude; a moment which has made the strongest pillars of sanctity tremble! St. Hilarion for 70 years had served God faithfully in the desert, separated from the society of men by a life of the most austere and unremitting penance; and yet he was obliged to comfort his spirit with those memorable words: "Depart, my soul, depart! What dost thou fear? For 70 years hast thou served Christ, and dost thou fear to die?" It is related of St. Andrew Avellino, that he had so fierce a combat at the hour of his death that his face was swollen and became black, he trembled in every limb, torrents of tears flowed from his eyes, and his head shook violently; and those present even wept for compassion, and at the same time trembled with fear, at the sight of so great a saint dying in such agony. What will become of us, who are loaded with sins, at that awful moment? Take courage, Parthenius; let us constantly love and faithfully serve Mary, and by her aid and assistance we shall happily pass through that awful trial. It is impossible for us to conceive what a great comfort and consolation it will be to us, at that moment, to have been devout and loving servants of this Most

Powerful Lady.

There are three things which torment the dying man: the past, the present, and the future. The past torments by the bitter remembrance of sins committed, of sinful omissions, and obligations neglected or despised. At that moment they all crowd before the sight of the dying man. "I now remember," said the wicked king, Antiochus, "I now remember all the evil which I have done." The evil one will not neglect to exaggerate their weight and circumstances by the most lively representation possible. The certainty of the sins committed, and the uncertainty of pardon, place the soul in an agony of despair. But if we constantly and fervently love Mary, she will obtain for us the grace to make our peace with God beforehand by a good confession, true contrition, and a sincere and efficacious resolution to amend our life, so that we may then joyfully sing with David: "As far as the east is from the west, so far hath he removed our iniquities from us." (*Psalm* 102:12). The confident hope and probable certainty of pardon, will then be to us the greatest comfort and consolation, reminding us of the words of God: "Their sins and iniquities I will remember no more." (*Hebrews* 10:17).

And she will obtain for us at that moment such great contrition and sorrow for our sins, that there will spring up in our heart a moral certainty that her intercession has obtained for us the mercy of God. She will not fail to infuse into our heart such great hope and confidence in the goodness of God, and in her efficacious mediation, that we shall be filled with joy and content. She has obtained for many, even at the last moment, a most lively sorrow for their sins, and has thus saved them and has carried comfort in her own person to many who feared and trembled at the remembrance of their sins.

The present torments the dying man by the sufferings of the body, joined to the temptations and furious assaults of our common enemy, who then does his worst, according to the words of the Apocalypse: "The devil is come down unto you having great wrath, knowing that he hath but a short time." (*Apoc.* 12:12). But let us not fear, Parthenius; Mary will be with us if we love her, she will comfort us, console us, and defend us.

Amid sorrows and afflictions she will obtain for us from the Lord such patience and resignation to the Divine Will, that besides the great merit we shall acquire by suffering, our very pains will become a most sweet consolation to us, as we reflect on the benefit they are to us, by purifying our soul, and thereby lessening the future torments which we might be condemned to in Purgatory. I do not say that she will grant us those little sensible proofs of affection which she has given to some of the saints; but she will find a way to console and relieve us, even in our greatest troubles and infirmities, according to the words of Wisdom: "Them that love her, she shall deliver from their troubles"; and as she said to Saint Bridget, like a most kind mistress and mother she will visit those who love her, and give them comfort and ease at the hour of their death. *(Revel. St. Bridget, lib. 1, cap. 29).* Hell will then rise up against us with all its power and fury, and make a last effort to conquer us, but Mary will defend us, and "if she is for us who will be against us?"

We may sing with the prophet: "Though I should walk in the midst of the shadow of death I will fear no evils, for thou art with me." (*Psalm* 22:4). She will be "terrible as an army in battle array" to defend us against our enemies; they that hate us shall fly before her face, and be dissipated and scattered like dust before the wind, when she arises for our defense; for after the example of her Son, she preserves the souls of her servants, and will deliver them from the hands of the wicked, and out of the power of the evil one. The Holy Ghost, knowing what a good protection she is to us, gives us that most excellent advice: "Forsake her not, and she shall keep thee: love her, and she shall preserve thee." (*Prov.* 4:6). "Glorious and wonderful, O Mary, is thy name," says Saint Bonaventure; "they that invoke it shall not tremble at the hour of death; for the devils retreat from the soul when they hear the name of Mary." *(In Psalt.).* "She sends the angels with the prince of the heavenly hosts, Saint Michael, to defend and receive the souls of her servants, who confidently invoke her." *(In Spec. c. 3).*

And not satisfied with this, she comes herself to their assistance at the hour of death, and receives the souls of her children, in order to present them herself to God. Such was the death of Saint Andrew Avellino, of which we have already spoken. After the fierce conflict with Hell, in which by the assistance of Mary he was victorious, the pains of his body ceased; his face resumed its usual appearance, and with his eyes fixed on the image of Mary, he devoutly bowed his head in reverence and thanksgiving to her, and calmly gave up his soul into her hands. When Father Manuel was dying, Mary appeared to him, and a host of demons were seen to retreat in despair, saying, "We can do nothing to him because she who is Immaculate, defends him."

Galeazzo Gabrielli, who entered our congregation, and was called Father Peter of Fano, enriched it with a number of benefices which he had enjoyed and which he renounced in its favor, as well as by his rare example of virtue and penance. At his last hour he was terribly assaulted by his infernal enemies; but being assisted by Mary, he overcame them and exclaimed: "I have conquered! I have conquered!" and began to recite the *Te Deum laudamus,* which was continued by the religious who were present, and in the middle of it he expired.

Lastly, the future terrifies us by the horror of death, the fear of approaching Judgment, and the doubt of our salvation. But praise be to God, and to His Most Holy Mother, and blessed be the servitude of love which we profess for her, who is Our Hope, Our Advocate, and Our Consolation! So great, in that moment, will be the consolation and sweetness which she will infuse into our soul, so great our trust in her protection and defense, and so great our hope and certainty of salvation, that death will seem a sweet repose after our fatigues, and we shall regard the destruction of our body as the fall of a prison, whose ruin sets us at liberty; we shall look at the approaching Judgment as a favorable decision of our cause, with Mary the Mother of our Judge for our solicitor, and the sentence of the Judge as a complete triumph, which is to put us in possession of eternal happiness.

Happy shall we then be to be bound in her chains, for "her chains bind to salvation"; they will be to us chains of peace, happiness, and consolation, for they make our salvation certain, and give to death the peace and consolation which is the commencement of eternal repose. "For in the latter end thou shalt find rest in her, and she shall be turned to thy joy. Then shall her fetters be a strong defense for thee, and a firm foundation, and her chain a robe of glory." (*Ecclus.* 6:29, 30). The great Suarez exclaimed when dying, "I did not think it was so sweet to die!" He died happily, for he loved Mary; and he used to say that all his wisdom was not worth the merit of one "Hail Mary." Another devout child of Mary said to Father Binetti, who was present at his death, "O Father, if you only knew how happy I am for having served and loved Mary! I cannot express the joy I feel at this moment." *(P. Binetti, Perf. Mar. c. 31).*

To Saint John of God she said, "I am not one of those who abandon their friends at the hour of death" *(Bolland. March 8th);* but, as she said to Saint Matilda, "Like a most affectionate mother, I am always present at the death of those who serve me, in order to console and protect them." *(Apud Blos. p. ii. Concl. An. Fid. a. 12).*

If, then, we love and faithfully serve Mary, we shall find that at the hour of death, the recollection of our sins will not afflict us, but we shall be consoled in the midst of the horrors of death, and conquer the furious assaults of our enemies; we shall not fear the Judgment, but certain of our salvation, we shall calmly deliver our soul into the hands of Mary, Our Most Loving Mother.

This is my hope, Most Sweet Mother, and I know that they that have hoped in thee have never been confounded. Shall I be the first? No! Thy word shall not fail, nor thy all-powerful mercy.

"O Most Sweet Mother and Especial Refuge of Sinners, Only Comforter of the Afflicted, Most Powerful and Most Merciful Lady; may I merit at the hour of death to enjoy thy presence, to taste and know the sweets of thy mercy! Make me feel the extent and power of thy kindness, strengthen me against all temptation, excuse my sins to thy Son, and through the merits of the sufferings of my Redeemer, and thy own afflictions, conduct my soul into life everlasting." *(Lanspergius).*

Twenty-Ninth Day

AFTER DEATH MARY WILL BE OUR ADVOCATE AT THE JUDGMENT, OUR COMFORT IN PURGATORY, AND, AFTER GOD, OUR BEATITUDE IN HEAVEN

Happy, Parthenius, are they who love Mary; they are prospered in life, assisted and consoled by her in the hour of death, and protected, delivered, and blessed after death. Death is a fixed barrier where the favor, protection, and love of human creatures terminate; they cannot pass over it, and extend beyond the confines of time into eternity.

But Mary's love reaches beyond the narrow limits which confine the affection of man's heart; her protection continues after death; she defends us at the Judgment, relieves us in Purgatory, and, after God, constitutes our happiness for eternity.

She will be Our Most Powerful Advocate and Defense, in the exact account which we shall have to render to God after our death. At that most minute scrutiny of all our least thoughts, words, and actions, all will be weighed in the scales of the sanctuary, and woe to him who is found wanting in weight. "I will search Jerusalem with lamps." (*Sophon.* 1).

> "What shall guilty I then plead?
> Who for me will intercede,
> When the saints shall comfort need?"
> *(—Dies Irae)*

Mary will then defend us, if we love her now. She will be our advocate at the bar of Divine Justice. "O wonderful effect of God's mercy towards us!" exclaims Saint Bonaventure *(In Salve. Reg.);* "Lest we should be frightened at the thought of His judgments, He gives us His Mother to be Our Advocate." And this, Our Advocate, is not only strong and powerful to gain whatever cause she pleads, but she is also so kind and loving that she will refuse to intercede for no one.

With reason does Saint Denis the Carthusian call her "the Especial Refuge of the Miserable, the Hope and Advocate of Sinners." Mary said to the venerable sister Maria Villani, "Next to the title of Mother of God, I glory most in being called the Refuge of Sinners." We must appear before a Just and Rigorous Judge, before a Supreme and Inexorable Tribunal, but our cause is in the hands of a Most Loving and Powerful Advocate. With her to defend me, I do not fear to appear before the judgment-seat of God; for no one will dare to accuse me when they see her stand up to protect me. Though all men, and all the saints and angels should demand my condemnation, and Mary should ask for my salvation, she is sure to be heard. Even the devils themselves confessed this to Saint Dominic, as is related by Paciucchelli.

After we have gained the great cause of our eternal salvation through the protection of Mary, we have still to satisfy Divine Justice for those faults from which we have not been wholly purged in this life, since nothing defiled can enter into Heaven, but must be purified by the fire of Purgatory. But do not believe, Parthenius, that Our Loving Mother will forget us then, and abandon us to our sufferings and the punishment of our sins. But rather, as our need of her assistance will then be the greater, as we cannot then help ourselves, so also will her pity and compassion for us be the greater, and she will be wholly occupied in consoling and relieving us.

She will not cease to raise her supplications to the throne of Divine Mercy; she will send the angels to comfort and relieve us; she will inspire the living to assist us with their prayers, and will sometimes obtain for us permission to appear upon earth to ask help from our friends, as she did for Innocent III, who appeared to Saint Ludgardes and said to her: "That I am permitted to come and ask your prayers, is owing to the intercession of the Mother of Mercy." She sometimes visits the souls in Purgatory in her own person, in order to console them, and she is continually engaged in obtaining their liberation. As she declared to Saint Bridget, "I am the Mother of all who are in Purgatory, and by my prayers their pains are constantly lightened; for there is no suffering in Purgatory which I do not render easy to bear." *(Rev. l. 4, c. 132).* "Those who are in Purgatory rejoice when they hear my name, like a dying man when he hears some word of hope." *(Ibid. l. 1, 116).*

But this Most Kind Mother is not satisfied with refreshing, consoling, and assisting these her most dear children; she wishes also to see them out of their prison, and offers to her Son her merits, and to the Eternal Father the merits of her Son, that their sufferings may be made lighter, and their punishment shorter. Gerson says, with many learned authors, that Our Most Merciful Lady, being about to ascend to Heaven on the day of her glorious Assumption, begged of her Divine Son to be allowed to deliver, and take with her to glory, all the souls who were then in Purgatory, so that she left it entirely empty.

Saint Denis the Carthusian asserts that every year,

on Christmas and Easter, the Blessed Virgin descends to Purgatory, accompanied by a multitude of angels, and delivers many of the souls confined there. *(Mund. Mar. part 2, d. 1, n. 45).* Saint Peter Damian thinks that the same also happens on all the feasts of the Blessed Virgin. Well-known is the promise which the Holy Virgin made to Pope John XXII, that she would deliver from Purgatory, on the first Saturday after their death, all those who wore the scapular of Mount Carmel, as was declared by him in his bull, which was confirmed by Alexander V, Clement VII, Saint Pius V, Gregory XIII, and Paul V. Innumerable are the instances of souls of the dead appearing to the living, and testifying that they were delivered from Purgatory by the intercession of the Most Holy Virgin.

Such is the care which Our Blessed Lady takes of all those souls in Purgatory; but still greater is her solicitude for her faithful servants, who tenderly loved her in life. "See," says Novarinus, "what advantage it is to love Mary, who does not forget the sufferings of her servants in Purgatory; and although she brings help and rest to all, she takes more especial care of those who were devout to her." *(Excit. 86).*

Not only does this Loving Queen of Mercy console her children, and quickly deliver them from Purgatory, but she often obtains for them an entire remission of that punishment, so that, purified in this life, they pass directly to Heaven. It is true that this is very rare, since we read of many saints who, for their small faults, which they did not even know, were not exempted from passing through Purgatory. Still it is not impossible, and we shall obtain it if we are very devout lovers of Mary; if we do penance for our past transgressions; if frequently making acts of contrition, we carefully guard against venial sins, especially those done with deliberation; if we make our confessions with sincerity, minuteness, and sorrow, and lose no occasion to gain holy indulgences.

This is the certain way, these are the sure means to avoid those pains; and if we love Mary, and often pray for this grace, she will not fail to obtain it from God, to enable us to do the aforesaid things, and to be most intensely sorry for our faults at the hour of our death, that, we being thus well purged in this life, she may conduct us directly to paradise. This is a grace which she has obtained for many, as for blessed Godfrey, to whom she sent Brother Abondio with this message: "Say to Brother Godfrey, to go on in virtue, making himself agreeable and pleasing to my Son and me; and when his soul shall leave his body, it shall not pass through Purgatory, but I will carry it and offer it to my Son." *(In lib. de Gest. Ill. Vol. Villard).*

Finally, Our Most Amiable Lady will be our glory and beatitude, after God, in paradise. And who can express the glory and delight with which she will honor and bless her servants and lovers? They will have a particular mark which will increase their glory, and distinguish them from all others as the special servants of Mary; "for all her domestics are clothed with double garments." *(Prov.* 31:21). They will be decorated with a double garment of glory; for besides the glory which is possessed by all the blessed, they will have the additional glory of having been the faithful lovers and servants of Mary; and this is so great an honor that Saint John Damascen says: "It is the greatest glory to serve Mary and be numbered among her domestics; for to serve her is to reign, and her slaves are greater than kings." *(De Excell. Virg.).* As the virgins follow the Lamb wherever He goes, so the servants and lovers of Mary will form her court, be always near her, and be distinguished by her especial affection. "It is the glorious privilege of the glory of Mary," says St. Bonaventure *(In Spec. B. V., c. v. pr. 7.),* "that whatever is sweetest and most delightful in paradise is Mary, is in Mary, and is by Mary." Our greatest glory and happiness, after God, is Mary, as Bernard says: "The greatest glory, after God, is to see thee, O Mary, to be close to thee, and to repose under the shadow of thy protection." O happy lovers, most fortunate servants of Mary, behold how your love will terminate in an eternal, immense fullness of glory and blessedness, which no man shall take from you! After prospering you in body and soul through life; after assisting and consoling you in death; defending and saving you after death, she makes you most blessed and glorious in Heaven, for all eternity.

Who will not love thee, O Mary? He only who knows thee not. Who can there be that does not know thee, since the sound of thy praises has gone forth into all the earth? Who is there that does not see thee, who art the Sun that enlightens every man? He only who is blind, and wishes to continue so. Let not this be our fate, after so much light which thou hast poured into our souls, and so many favors which thou hast conferred upon us; suffer us not to lose the benefit of them all by adding to all our other sins that of perverse and voluntary blindness.

Thirtieth Day

EPILOGUE AND RECAPITULATION OF
THE WHOLE WORK

I am now approaching the end of this work. At its commencement I undertook to present you an object worthy of you, worthy of your love, on which you might employ the whole force of your affection with the greatest pleasure and glory, and to the great advantage of all your interests—both temporal and spiritual—in life, in death, after death, and in eternity. This I have endeavored to do to the extent of my poor ability, and of the lights which I have received from the Eternal Wisdom, and from Mary, the Mother of Wisdom. Whether I have succeeded to a certain extent, I know not; but this I know, that though I had all the tongues of men and angels, and all their wisdom, I could never describe the fullness of her perfections and sanctity.

I have endeavored to lay before you, one by one, some of the amiable qualities of Our Holy Mother; but in this chapter I wish to sum them all up, just as one who is trying to draw a human body, first begins with the members, and one by one draws all the parts of the body, and then, at last, unites them all together in due proportion and symmetry, and the whole body is formed.

Mary is, in herself, the Most Perfect and Amiable Object that can be found, outside of God; for in her are found all the perfections and graces which make her most pleasing to us and most deserving of all our love.

If, before throwing away our heart and affections, we would reason and reflect on the great essential imperfections which are found in other creatures, we would not be so prodigal of our love. We lament their inconstancy, while we should rather wonder that it is not greater than it is. This instability is seen by the light which shows the defects in the object beloved, which were before concealed by passion. But not so with Mary. The more she is known, the more amiable does she appear; and the more we contemplate her, the more do we discover her beautiful prerogatives and immense perfections, and feel ourselves still more inflamed with this celestial fire.

If our vanity and ambition elevate us and make us look for nobility and greatness, who is nobler and greater than Mary, in whose veins flows the blood of so many patriarchs, prophets, priests, and monarchs; whose flesh and blood are the Flesh and Blood of the True God; who is truly the Mother, the Daughter, and the Spouse of God? Since she has been elevated to so great dignity that she has no superior but God, all other creatures, the mighty princes and rulers of this world, and the glorious hierarchy of Heaven, are her subjects. Her throne is at the right hand of her Son, where she sits as the Mistress and Dispenser of all the treasures of the Divinity. But with such great dignity and elevation, she unites such humility, condescension, and affability, that she lowers herself to be the sister of her lovers, and the servant of her servants.

Do we need an authority and protection to shield us from Divine Justice, to preserve us from the miseries and calamities of nature or fortune, from the snares and persecutions of our visible or invisible enemies?

Mary is for us an Impenetrable Shield, a Most Strong Tower, and her authority and almost infinite power extend to Heaven, over the earth, and into Hell, commanding and ruling nature and fortune, and all creatures, demons, men and angels, and even God Himself, who glories in obeying her. Do we need counsel in our doubts, light in the darkness of our ignorance, a guide through the dangerous pilgrimage of this life? She is the Seat and Mother of Wisdom, who clears up our doubts, enlightens our ignorance, and conducts us safely to our home, to the haven of eternal life.

If in our association with men we are annoyed and disgusted by their natural or moral defects and imperfections, we have the company, the familiarity of Mary, who is all sweetness and perfection. Enriched at the first instant of her Immaculate Conception with an immense capital of grace, she has multiplied and increased it beyond all human calculation. There are no bounds to her charity, sweetness, gratitude, love, and munificence. "Oh! Blessed are thy men and blessed are thy servants, who stand before thee always and hear thy wisdom."

Ravished by human beauty, we are for a time transported beyond ourselves, losing all sense and reason in admiration of the beauty of the beloved; but it soon passes away, languishes, dies, and becomes a prey to worms and corruption. The beauty of Mary, when in this world, surpassed that of all women who ever lived, and now glorified and made immortal in Heaven, it constitutes a paradise of unending beatitude.

If riches are the object of our desires, in Mary are contained all the riches of nature and grace. All the gifts of God pass through her hands: as Saint Bernard

(Serm. de Nat.) says, "He has wished us to have everything from the hands of Mary." Rich beyond all conception of man, in every kind of wealth, she is most ready to bestow on us all that we ask of her; and even without waiting to be asked, at every moment, she loads us with her favors and benefits.

There remains but one drawback to our love, in the fear that one so noble, so beautiful, so powerful, and so rich, must care little for us, or for our love. However true this is in worldly love, where affection and union between those of unequal ranks is rare and wondered at, it is not so with Mary. She goes around diligently seeking for lovers, and says to them: "My son, give me thy heart, and I will give thee mine." She loves us with an insuperable and invincible love; more than all the mothers, sisters, and lovers in the world. Her love for us is only equalled by her love for God, and as she loves God more than all the angels and saints, more than all creatures, so also her love for us is greater than that of all other created beings. We might almost say, she loves us more than she does her Divine Son, since for love of us she sacrificed Him to the most barbarous death of the cross. If we measure her love by the extent of the benefits she has given us, here too we are overcome by the greatness of her affection. She daily and hourly enriches us with temporal and spiritual graces, notwithstanding our cold ingratitude and continual infidelity. But when she finds someone who corresponds to such great love, endeavoring to love and honor her in return, who can tell the strength, extent, force, constancy, and tenderness of her gratitude?

Oh, then, indeed, her "love is as strong as death," and even stronger, extending beyond time into eternity! But if such great amiability and love do not affect us, we shall at least be moved by our own interest and advantage. We appear to place all our happiness in these three things—honor, pleasure, and interest; by these three things our heart is carried away, but in the love of Mary we shall find all three united in the most perfect degree. What honor, what glory could be greater than to love and be loved by the greatest of all created beings? A being who by her most holy counsel, her authority, her power, and her protection, renders us wise, prudent, holy, and respectable before the world, and before Heaven? A being who takes upon herself the care of our reputation, preserving it if we have it, and even regaining it when we have lost it by our own fault? Profane love makes us insane and contemptible, but the love of Mary makes us honored and glorious.

Not less are pleasure and content found in the love of Mary. We know that our love of Mary is not contrary to the love of God, but that He approves it and desires it; and that it is a pleasant and secure path to sanctity and to Heaven; we know that it is a certain sign and secure pledge of our predestination and eternal salvation; we know that we love and are loved in return by a Lady who is all great, noble, powerful, wise, good, beautiful, rich, liberal, and courteous, and who takes such great care of us that it seems as though she thought of nothing else but how to make us happy in life and blessed after death. Does not such a soul swim in an ocean of content and pleasure? Free from all restlessness, rivalry, suspicion, and jealousy, which are the torment of the foolish lovers of the world, what rest, peace, and delight will we not, on the contrary, enjoy?

Finally, the interest and advantage, both temporal and spiritual, which we derive from the love of Mary, are immense, and beyond all conception. She is able and willing to give us, with a liberal hand, all the goods of nature, fortune, and grace, of which we stand in need. She distributes riches, honors, and dignities. All the graces of God are in her hands, and she freely bestows them upon us, even before we can ask for them. If we are just, she preserves us in justice and obtains for us new lights, new gifts, new graces, new merits. If we are sinners, she appeases the anger of God, suspends His punishments, and pressing us to her bosom, wards off the blows of His just indignation. She moderates the passions, preserves us from the dangers and occasions of sins, and restrains the fury of our spiritual enemies, so that we are less tempted and sin less grievously. She bursts the bonds of our passions and breaks the chains of our vices and evil habits; she delivers us from the slavery of the devil, and reclaims us even from the brink of Hell, and with amiable violence forces us to be converted, and obtains our pardon from God. She shortens, lessens, or takes away entirely the temporal punishment of our sins in this life, or obtains for us the grace to bear it with patience.

After we have escaped all the rocks and shoals, and storms of the tempestuous ocean of this life, she brings us safely to the port of our eternal salvation, assisting us in death that we may not be driven to despair by the recollection of our past offences, that we may suffer with patience and resignation the pains and agony of our last illness, that we may boldly resist and finally conquer the last efforts of Hell, and that we may not fear the approaching judgment, nor despair of our eternal salvation. After death she defends our cause as a powerful advocate, and with her patronage we are sure of gaining it; she relieves and consoles us in our sufferings in Purgatory; and delivering us from that prison of torments, or sometimes not even permitting us to go there, she conducts us to eternal glory, where, honoring us with the mark of her faithful lovers, she puts us in possession of God and eternal beatitude. Is it not then true, as Jordan says, that "if we find the Virgin, we find all that is good"? Does not he that possesses her, possess in the most eminent and perfect degree, without any defect or imperfection, all that is capable of captivating the heart?

But that which completes the incomprehensible loveliness of so worthy an object and so fortunate a love, is, that no accident, no power can separate us from it against our will. We shall enjoy it forever, we shall possess it eternally. No object in this world, to which we can attach our heart, will render us entirely happy and contented; it may be taken from us in a thousand ways. Created beauty is a beauty of a day, years waste both body and soul; a thousand accidents may separate us from the object of our affection, or deprive us of its love—or death may separate us forever. Il Ki, emperor of China, after erecting to his departed consort a gorgeous mausoleum, fell in love with another princess, and in the midst of his delight, as he gazed on his new bride, he burst into tears, exclaiming, "Can I not then, with all my power, give thee a life more durable than that of the least of my subjects? This bitter thought poisons all my happiness!" So true it is, as Saint Augustine says, that no happiness is perfect which is not lasting and immortal; and that only is true and solid joy which no one can take from us.

I now no longer wonder that they who know thee, Most Amiable Mary, are transported with love for thee; that Saint Bernardine of Sienna called thee his

Beloved; Saint Philip Neri, his Delight; Saint Stanislaus, his Mother; Blessed Herman, his Beloved Spouse; Saint Bonaventure, his Heart and his Soul; and Saint Bernard, Captivator of Hearts; that Saint Francis of Selano, intoxicated with love for thee, danced and sang songs of love before thy images; that Francis Beiranzio, Augustine Spinosa, and many others, wrote thy name with red-hot irons on their breast; and that Alphonsus Rodriguez, and a thousand others, wished to give their blood and their life as a proof of their love for thee; for thou art the delight and the joy of men and angels and of God.

And shall we, Parthenius, be of the number of those who throw away their love on a disgraceful object, which deprives them of honor, of peace, of rest, of content, of health, of life, of Heaven, and of God, rather than be consumed with the heavenly fire of the love of Mary, which will clothe us with glory, with pleasure, and with joy, and render us most content in life, most secure in death, and most happy in eternity?

No; we will love thee, Most Beautiful, Most Amiable of all creatures, with our whole heart and with our whole soul. Thou alone, after God, shalt be the center and the end of all our thoughts, of all our desires, and of all our affections. We will love thee faithfully, constantly, and eternally, and nothing shall ever separate us from thee—neither death, nor life, nor any creature. We therefore pray thee to bless these our resolutions, and to strengthen them, so that we may merit to enjoy thy love here on earth, and for all eternity in Heaven.

Thirty-First Day

WHAT WE MUST DO TO LOVE MARY

You must now be persuaded, Parthenius, and resolved to consecrate yourself to the love of God and that of His Most Holy Mother, the Mother of Fair Love. But you will now ask me what you must do to love Mary, and how you must love her. I am not now going to propose to you the many practices of devotion, and pious and holy exercises, which are performed by the devout lovers of Mary. I shall propose to you but one practice and exercise, which, according to my opinion, includes them all, and is a continual exercise of tender, sincere, and affectionate love. I will tell it to you in a few words, and if you faithfully practice it, I assure you that in a very short time you will become a saint, and a great saint, by a most easy and pleasant way.

I propose to you to imitate the foolish lovers of the world. They carefully guard against the least thing which might displease or offend, and endeavor to do everything to please and delight the person loved. They willingly suffer any pain, in order to give her pleasure or avoid displeasing her.

Now this is precisely what we must do if we truly wish to love Mary. Can we do less? And what kind of love would ours be if we should do otherwise? Can we truly say that we love her if we do that which displeases her, or omit that which may give her pleasure, or refuse to suffer anything for her sake? Such a love would be a manifest contradiction. Let us not suffer the lovers of this world to be wiser than the lovers of Heaven.

First, they guard against the least thing which might displease the one they love. They know that if they do anything to offend her, her love for them will grow cold, or be turned to aversion. They even try to conceal their defects, both natural and moral, which might diminish her esteem for them. Shall we pretend to love Mary, and yet take no care to avoid those things which offend her? Those things which displease and provoke God and His Divine Son? Her interests are so closely united with those of God and of her Son that they cannot be separated, and he that sins against God touches her in the pupil of the eye, and pierces her heart. Strange and barbarous would be the love of one who, while pretending to love the Mother and making known to her his love with the most affectionate expressions, should stab her only Son in her arms. Such, precisely, is our love if, while we profess to love Mary, we offend her Son, her Father, and her Spouse.

The lovers of this world not only guard carefully against offending the one they love, they also hold in the highest esteem and regard everything connected with the beloved. Let us guard against all that can offend God and we shall be sure not to displease Mary. And, as she penetrates to the bottom of our heart and sees all our thoughts, affections, and desires, hears all our words, and is present at all our actions, so that nothing is hidden from her, we must take care even of our least and most secret thoughts and actions which can offend her; and, especially, we should guard against fostering any love inconsistent with, or contrary to, her love. She is jealous, and will not suffer another to share our love; she desires it entirely for herself.

But the lovers of this world are not satisfied with not offending the object of their love; they also endeavor, by every means in their power, to cause it joy and pleasure. They would wish to foresee its desires in order to anticipate them. It is sufficient for them to know what will give the beloved pleasure, and, however hard or difficult, they fly to perform it. Should we do less than they? Shall we do nothing for so Amiable and Loving a Lady? We know what will please her, and what she desires of us, and shall we not be willing to do it? Her will is so united to that of her Holy Son, that they are but one and the same will; therefore, the greatest pleasure and satisfaction we can give her, is in the fulfillment of the divine commands, the counsels of her Son, and the obligations of our state in life. "Love is not idle," says Saint Gregory *(Hon. L. in Evang.);* "if it refuses to labor, it is not love."

"If you love me, keep my commandments. He that hath my commandments, and keepeth them; he it is that loveth me. And he that loveth me, shall be loved of my Father: and I will love him, and will manifest myself to him. He that loveth me not, keepeth not my words." *(Jn.* 14:15, 21 and 24). This is true love, and the most acceptable practice of devotion. If we keep the commandments of her Son, all other practices and exercises of devotion towards her are good and holy, but if they are not accompanied and united with this they cannot be called true love, nor be so acceptable to her as this. Let us make this our chief care and our only endeavor, with the motive and intention of pleasing her and God at the same time, and I assure you that she will accept with the greatest satisfaction this most sincere and convincing proof of our love, and will manifest herself to us in the fullness of her tender affection.

Lovers also endeavor to imitate and make themselves like to her they love, in disposition and habit, and even copy in themselves all her defects and peculiarities. Saint Gregory Nazianzen, as quoted by Saint Francis de Sales, relates that many persons loved Saint Basil to such a degree, as to endeavor to imitate him in his slow way of speaking, in his thoughtful and abstract manner, in the style of his beard, and his way of walking, and we daily see instances of this same effect of great love. This should be the endeavor of those who love Mary, and wish to give her pleasure. They should strive to imitate her, not in imperfections or defects, which cannot be found in her, but in her most noble virtues, especially those two which are the dearest to her—humility and purity. It is a maxim of philosophy that like loves and desires like; how tenderly then must Mary love those in whom she sees the image of her dearest virtues, those who try to imitate her in what they know she most loves!

In short, we must love Mary, and she will teach us what we are to do to gain her love and prove ours; she will teach us to remember her frequently, to make continual acts of love for her, to salute her often with the Angelical Salutation which is so dear to her, to invoke her in danger, in trouble and in difficulty, and to imitate her in all our actions. She will also teach us to venerate with special affection her holy images, to keep holy her feasts, and to worship her spouse, her holy parents, and the saints who are dearest to her; to recite with tender devotion prayers in her honor; and to place in her hands all our interests, our life, our health, and our hope. "True love," says Saint Laurence Justinian *(S. Laur. Justian. De Casto Connub. F. 150)*, "is not content with one degree, but strives always to obtain the higher and more perfect. Love is nourished with love, love feeds on itself, so that the more it loves the more it desires to love."

The love of Mary is not like the love of other creatures, which is satisfied and weakened by the possession and enjoyment of the object loved; but the more we love her the more we desire to love her, according to the saying of Ecclesiasticus, "They that eat me shall yet hunger; and they that drink me shall yet thirst." *(Ecclus.* 24:29).

Finally, lovers suffer not only patiently but with joy every inconvenience and fatigue, for the sake of the beloved. Cabala, one of the greatest lords of Byzantium, in order to gain the favor of a lady whom he wished to marry, and who refused him because he was too fat, put himself under the care of physicians and was subjected to a most painful course of treatment, being deprived of food and sleep, and obliged to exercise his body with great labor, in order to get rid of his odious fatness, and make himself pleasing in the eyes of his beloved. *(Byov. A.D. 1342).* And shall we refuse to suffer anything for the love of Mary, who asks of us nothing hard or difficult, but only what is easy and delightful? Her love is a paradise of delight, a fountain of pleasure and eternal life, celestial nectar, and the joy of the just. It is a consolation which sweetens every difficulty and lightens every burden: "For her conversation hath no bitterness, nor her company any tediousness, but joy and gladness. And there is great delight in her friendship, and inexhaustible riches in the works of her hands, and in the exercise of conference with her, wisdom, and glory in the communication of her words: and I went about seeking that I might take her to myself." (*Wis.* 8:16, 18).

This is the true exercise of love for her and the most certain proof we can give her of our affection and tender devotion; it is also the way to become great saints. It is the shortest, most certain, and at the same time least laborious, but rather, pleasant and easy way to arrive at great perfection, and obtain our eternal salvation. All the other ways are good and holy, but they are difficult and narrow, for they are either the way of innocence or of penance, while this is the way of love which sweetly and insensibly leads to God, the love of Mary being the love of God, and what is done for her is done for God. "The kingdom of heaven suffereth violence, and the violent bear it away." (*Matt.* 11:12). This violence consists in resisting the inclinations of nature, the snares of the world, the temptations of our most cunning enemy, the allurements of the senses and the irregularities of passion. This is hard and difficult to our corrupt nature, but the love of Mary makes it easy and pleasant, for she captivates our hearts to the service of God.

St. Mary Magdalen of Passi, rapt in an ecstasy, saw the Holy Virgin in a ship, in which, like an expert pilot, she guided those devout to her to eternal life. Brother Leo, one of the first companions of St. Francis, saw two ladders stretching from the earth to Heaven; at the top of one stood Jesus Christ looking serious and austere, and at the top of the other stood the Blessed Virgin with a sweet and amiable countenance. He also saw St. Francis there present, inviting all men, but particularly those of his order, to ascend to Heaven by the first ladder. But seeing that some fell at the commencement and others even fell from higher up, he told them to go to the other ladder, where, encouraged by the smiling appearance of the Holy Virgin, they easily ascended, and all, without exception, entered into Heaven. *(Fr. Plattus, Book 1, chapter 34).*

We are not to infer from this vision that Jesus Christ is not the true way to Heaven, for, as He says, He is the Way, the Truth, and the Life; but as in Him, besides the Redeemer, men also see the severe Judge, they might lack that true and loving confidence which they find in Mary, who is the Advocate and Mother of Mercy.

Let us enter, Parthenius, in this way. Let us ascend on this safe ladder. As says Thomas a Kempis, "Salute Mary, think of Mary, invoke Mary, honor Mary, commend yourselves to Mary, remain with Mary in your house, and walk with Mary when you go out; rejoice with Mary, grieve with Mary, work with Mary, pray with Mary; with Mary carry Jesus in your arms, stand with Mary at the foot of the cross of Jesus, live and die with Mary and Jesus. Do this and thou shalt live."

If you have enjoyed this book, consider making your next selection from among the following . . .

Prices guaranteed through December 31, 1995.

Miraculous Images of Our Lady. *Joan Carroll Cruz* 20.00
Brief Catechism for Adults. *Fr. Cogan* 9.00
Raised from the Dead. *Fr. Hebert* 15.00
Autobiography of St. Margaret Mary 4.00
Thoughts and Sayings of St. Margaret Mary 3.00
The Voice of the Saints. *Comp. by Francis Johnston* 5.00
The 12 Steps to Holiness and Salvation. *St. Alphonsus* . . 7.00
The Rosary and the Crisis of Faith. *Cirrincione/Nelson* . . 1.25
Sin and Its Consequences. *Cardinal Manning* 5.00
Fourfold Sovereignty of God. *Cardinal Manning* 5.00
Dialogue of St. Catherine of Siena. *Transl. Thorold* 9.00
Catholic Answer to Jehovah's Witnesses. *D'Angelo* 8.00
Twelve Promises of the Sacred Heart. (100 cards) 5.00
St. Aloysius Gonzaga. *Fr. Meschler* 10.00
The Love of Mary. *D. Roberto* 7.00
Begone Satan. *Fr. Vogl* 2.00
The Prophets and Our Times. *Fr. R. G. Culleton* 11.00
St. Therese, The Little Flower. *John Beevers* 4.50
Mary, The Second Eve. *Cardinal Newman* 2.50
Devotion to Infant Jesus of Prague. Booklet 75
The Wonder of Guadalupe. *Francis Johnston* 6.00
Apologetics. *Msgr. Paul Glenn* 9.00
Baltimore Catechism No. 1 . . . . 3.00
Baltimore Catechism No. 2 . . . . 4.00
Baltimore Catechism No. 3 . . . . 7.00
An Explanation of the Baltimore Catechism. *Kinkead* . . .13.00
Bible History. *Schuster* 10.00
Blessed Eucharist. *Fr. Mueller* 9.00
Catholic Catechism. *Fr. Faerber* 5.00
The Devil. *Fr. Delaporte* 5.00
Dogmatic Theology for the Laity. *Fr. Premm* 18.00
Evidence of Satan in the Modern World. *Cristiani* 8.50
Fifteen Promises of Mary. (100 cards) 5.00
Life of Anne Catherine Emmerich. 2 vols. *Schmoger* 37.50
Life of the Blessed Virgin Mary. *Emmerich* 15.00
Prayer to St. Michael. (100 leaflets) 5.00
Prayerbook of Favorite Litanies. *Fr. Hebert* 9.00
Preparation for Death. (Abridged). *St. Alphonsus* 7.00
Purgatory Explained. *Schouppe* 13.50
Purgatory Explained. (pocket, unabr.). *Schouppe* 9.00
Spiritual Conferences. *Tauler* 12.00
Trustful Surrender to Divine Providence. *Bl. Claude* 4.00
Wife, Mother and Mystic. *Bessieres* 7.00
The Agony of Jesus. *Padre Pio* 1.50

Prices guaranteed through December 31, 1995.

Catholic Home Schooling. *Mary Kay Clark* 15.00
The Cath. Religion—Illus. & Expl. *Msgr. Burbach* 9.00
Wonders of the Holy Name. *Fr. O'Sullivan* 1.50
How Christ Said the First Mass. *Fr. Meagher* 16.50
Too Busy for God? Think Again! *D'Angelo* 4.00
St. Bernadette Soubirous. *Trochu* 16.50
Passion and Death of Jesus Christ. *Liguori* 8.50
Treatise on the Love of God. 2 Vols. *de Sales* 16.50
Confession Quizzes. Radio Replies Press 1.00
St. Philip Neri. *Fr. V. J. Matthews* 4.50
St. Louise de Marillac. *Sr. Vincent Regnault* 4.50
The Old World and America. *Rev. Philip Furlong* 16.50
Prophecy for Today. *Edward Connor* 4.50
Bethlehem. *Fr. Faber* 16.50
The Book of Infinite Love. *Mother de la Touche* 4.50
The Church Teaches. Church Documents 15.00
Conversation with Christ. *Peter T. Rohrbach* 8.00
Purgatory and Heaven. *J. P. Arendzen* 3.50
Liberalism Is a Sin. *Sarda y Salvany* 6.00
Spiritual Legacy/Sr. Mary of Trinity. *van den Broek* 9.00
The Creator and the Creature. *Fr. Frederick Faber* 13.50
Radio Replies. 3 Vols. Frs. *Rumble and Carty* 36.00
Convert's Catechism of Catholic Doctrine. *Geiermann* . . . 3.00
Incarnation, Birth, Infancy of Jesus Christ. *Liguori* 8.50
Light and Peace. *Fr. R. P. Quadrupani* 5.00
Dogmatic Canons & Decrees of Trent, Vat. I. 8.00
The Evolution Hoax Exposed. *A. N. Field* 6.00
The Priest, the Man of God. *St. Joseph Cafasso* 12.00
Christ Denied. *Fr. Paul Wickens* 2.00
New Regulations on Indulgences. *Fr. Winfrid Herbst* 2.50
A Tour of the Summa. *Msgr. Paul Glenn* 18.00
Spiritual Conferences. *Fr. Frederick Faber* 13.50
Bible Quizzes. Radio Replies Press 1.00
Marriage Quizzes. Radio Replies Press 1.00
True Church Quizzes. Radio Replies Press 1.00
St. Lydwine of Schiedam. *J. K. Huysmans* 7.00
Mary, Mother of the Church. Church Documents 3.00
The Sacred Heart and the Priesthood. *de la Touche* 7.00
Blessed Sacrament. *Fr. Faber* 16.50
Revelations of St. Bridget. *St. Bridget of Sweden* 2.50
Magnificent Prayers. *St. Bridget of Sweden* 1.50
The Happiness of Heaven. *Fr. J. Boudreau* 7.00
The Glories of Mary. *St. Alphonsus Liguori* 16.50
The Glories of Mary. (pocket, unabr.). *St. Alphonsus* . . . 9.00

Prices guaranteed through December 31, 1995.

Ven. Jacinta Marto of Fatima. *Cirrincione* 1.50
Reign of Christ the King. *Davies* 1.25
St. Teresa of Ávila. *William Thomas Walsh* 18.00
Isabella of Spain—The Last Crusader. *Wm. T. Walsh* 20.00
Characters of the Inquisition. *Wm. T. Walsh* 12.50
Philip II. *William Thomas Walsh.* H.B. 37.50
Blood-Drenched Altars—Cath. Comment. Hist. Mexico. . 18.00
Self-Abandonment to Divine Providence. *de Caussade* . . . 16.50
Way of the Cross. *Liguorian.* 75
Way of the Cross. *Franciscan* 75
Modern Saints—Their Lives & Faces, Bk. 1. *Ann Ball* . . . 18.00
Modern Saints—Their Lives & Faces, Bk. 2. *Ann Ball* . . 20.00
Saint Michael and the Angels. *Approved Sources* 5.50
Dolorous Passion of Our Lord. *Anne C. Emmerich* 15.00
Our Lady of Fatima's Peace Plan from Heaven. Booklet. .75
Divine Favors Granted to St. Joseph. *Pere Binet* 4.00
St. Joseph Cafasso—Priest of the Gallows. *St. J. Bosco* . . 3.00
Catechism of the Council of Trent. *McHugh/Callan* 20.00
Padre Pio—The Stigmatist. *Fr. Charles Carty* 13.50
Why Squander Illness? *Frs. Rumble & Carty* 2.00
Fatima—The Great Sign. *Francis Johnston* 7.00
Heliotropium—Conformity of Human Will to Divine 11.00
Charity for the Suffering Souls. *Fr. John Nageleisen* 15.00
Devotion to the Sacred Heart of Jesus. *Verheylezoon* 13.00
Sermons on Prayer. *St. Francis de Sales* 3.50
Sermons on Our Lady. *St. Francis de Sales* 9.00
Sermons for Lent. *St. Francis de Sales* 10.00
Fundamentals of Catholic Dogma. *Ott* 20.00
Litany of the Blessed Virgin Mary. (100 cards) 5.00
Who Is Padre Pio? Radio Replies Press 1.50
Child's Bible History. *Knecht* 4.00
The Life of Christ. 4 Vols. H.B. *Anne C. Emmerich* 55.00
St. Anthony—The Wonder Worker of Padua. *Stoddard* . . . 4.00
The Precious Blood. *Fr. Faber* 11.00
The Holy Shroud & Four Visions. *Fr. O'Connell* 2.00
Clean Love in Courtship. *Fr. Lawrence Lovasik* 2.50
The Secret of the Rosary. *St. Louis De Montfort* 3.00
The History of Antichrist. *Rev. P. Huchede* 3.00
Where We Got the Bible. *Fr. Henry Graham* 5.00
Hidden Treasure—Holy Mass. *St. Leonard* 4.00
Imitation of the Sacred Heart of Jesus. *Fr. Arnoudt* 13.50
The Life & Glories of St. Joseph. *Edward Thompson* . . . 13.50

At your bookdealer or direct from the publisher.

Prices guaranteed through December 31, 1995.